CONFESSIONS
OF A
CORPORATE
HEADHUNTER

CONFESSIONS OF A CORPORATE HEADHUNTER

BY ALLAN J. COX

TRIDENT PRESS *New York*

A portion of this manuscript in substantially altered form
appeared in the January 1972 issue of Playboy *magazine.*

Published by Trident Press
A division of Simon & Schuster, Inc.
Rockefeller Center, 630 Fifth Avenue
New York, New York 10020

SBN 671-27104-0
Library of Congress Catalog Card Number: 72-96812
Designed by Irving Perkins
Manufactured in the United States of America
Printed by The Murray Printing Company, Forge Village, Mass.
Bound by The Plimpton Press, Norwood, Mass.

1 2 3 4 5 6 7 8 9 10

Dedicated to my forbearing clients,
some of whom will recognize themselves in print,
and others, hopefully, who will not.

CONTENTS

PREFACE

Among the odd assortment of convictions and biases which shape my view of life are three reasons for my writing this book.

The first involves a benign compassion I hold for today's mobile executive. Knowing that his economic and emotional well-being are often dependent upon company caprice, I feel obliged to offer him my advice on coping with corporate wisdom.

It is true that as a professional my loyalty must go to the corporate client who foots my bill. But my *raw material* as an executive recruiter is the executive-in-transit whose longing for new challenges and a better life makes him susceptible to my siren song. I owe him a great deal because without him I and my profession could not exist.

Though in a moral sense my debt to him is large, it is not thought to be such in the business community generally. Accordingly, I am under no constraint to be of more than passing service to him. If he has what my corporate client needs, I am interested in him. If he does not, I'm not.

It is this kind of attitude among corporations and head-hunters alike that can subject the executive to an array of abuses, cause him grief, and even harm his career. This book may help him avoid becoming grist for the corporate mill.

The second reason for the book is narcissistic. In some small way I believe my observations will add to the understanding of corporate organization. In these pages I will make clear that some of us headhunters possess an awareness of interpersonal dynamics and group functioning which many clients have thought nonexistent. For example, my own style is that of an organizational consultant who has headhunting in his bag of tricks as but one way to help energize corporate bodies experiencing fatigue in one or more vital organs.

Clients often reorganize their companies, draw neat boxes on organization charts, put new names in those boxes, look confidently to the future—then discover things didn't go according to plan.

The problem in such cases is that the client hasn't understood the interpersonal processes among his executives, the hidden cliques, vanities, powerplays, prevarications and vested interests, which operate at cross-purposes with stated objectives. Ferreting out these sabotaging factors is an important part of corporate organization.

The first step is understanding what makes executives tick. And here the headhunter, by virtue of his experience, is an expert.

An experienced headhunter has seen hundreds of executives from hundreds of companies across the total range of American business. He has seen them in all basic industries. He has seen them in success and failure; economic ascent and decline; joy and sorrow; boredom and excitement; creativity and barrenness; in boom times and recession; drunk and sober; frightened and confident.

Some men will lie, steal and cheat while others give altruistically of themselves without thought of reward. The headhunter has seen them all—the brilliant and the dull; the effective and the incompetent; the glib and the inarticulate; the energetic and the lazy; those from influential families and the right schools and those from the wrong side of the tracks.

In short, he knows the executive mind and being; what stimulates executives and what doesn't. He also learns to spot those who probably can't be stimulated in business at all—who should be encouraged to make a living somewhere else.

As a headhunter, I frequently am asked to find executives for companies that don't need them at all, the right executives for the wrong jobs or the wrong executives for the right jobs. Because such activities generate enormous wastes of time, energy, brainpower and money, I hope my insights will help those concerned with organization planning and the problem-solving process. After all, my ultimate concern is understanding and improving organizational processes, not just filling holes in organization charts.

The third reason has to do with presenting a challenge to contemporary business. While it may be draining to listen to uninformed idealists who blame business for most of society's ills, American corporations do have to reorder their priorities.

In the final section of the book I urge the corporation to see its place in the world in a new light. Actually this call to a fresh outlook is not so much a challenge as encouragement; optimistic support for its changing role in society at large. Such optimism is based on growing corporate concern over its social-environmental villainy, dehumanization, rigidity toward new executive life-styles, and unattractiveness to the young. Happily, enlightened members of the business establishment are themselves convinced that the corporation must be concerned with more than mere production of goods and services.

But good intentions and uninformed idealism will not do. Indeed they can even prove harmful. Consequently, in my assessment of corporate dysfunctions I have tried to be realistic. Façades, though less intentional among the sincere, are just as present and real as among the sinister. I have tried to see behind the façade; to anticipate fruitless outcomes for well-intentioned programs and actions.

So the following caveat is in order: Anyone reading this book for support of a radical remaking of the corporation will be disappointed. Actually, my own thinking runs counter to radicalism. This is not because I am conservative, but because I hope to see behind the façade. Seeing behind the façade shatters illusions, and it should be remembered that illusions not only nourish aspects of business as usual, they also nurture utopian fervor.

Special thanks go to my wife, Bonnie, who offered encouragement and nobly endured my moods throughout this project. In addition, my secretary, Kathryn L. Sentman, is to be commended for her stoicism in the face of picayune requests and repeated typing of the manuscript. Clients and job candidates are hereby accorded my heartfelt gratefulness because without them there would be no observational field on which to report. What's more, I would be out of work!

ALLAN J. COX

Chicago, Illinois

"No. I don't recommend him; but I point him out."

——A Man for All Seasons (*Thomas More making a graceful but important distinction in discussing a job aspirant*)

I. "CONFESSIONS"

As an executive recruiter I often know where exciting jobs paying upward of $50,000 are for the taking. I know the corporations that are searching for the executives; I know the best way to impress management; and, finally, I usually know if it's in a candidate's best interest to accept an offer.

Superficially, these attainments make me an attractive person to know, and, were it not that the profession I practice is probably the most opportunistic, cynical, defensive, and manipulative of the corporate-service industries, I would humbly agree with such a self-congratulatory assessment.

I believe that I have been well served by having come to the executive recruitment profession with a properly worldly attitude to the world of business and what my function in it could be.

At college, I set my goals to be a social psychologist and professor. I did my homework, earned an advanced degree, and soon realized my collegiate ambition by joining the sociology faculty of a small, quality, midwestern liberal arts college. I taught courses in social psychology, sociological theory, and social disorganization, and began working on a doctorate. While several of my friends entered the business world and received my youthful scorn, I set out to make what I, at the time, deemed a "really important" contribution. I would be a writer, a teacher, a molder of the young, dispensing droplets of existential relevance to their blotterlike minds and beings.

My story is a common one; I'll relate it only briefly. Academia proved as cutthroat as the floor of the Chicago commodity exchange. Faculty and administrative infighting was something to behold, while my students were on the whole about as resistant to enlightment as Attila the Hun. I also got fed up with being poor. I declined the opportunity to complete my doctorate at the University of Colorado, and when the chance came for me to join a management-consulting firm and make good use of my theoretical training as a staff psychologist and personnel consultant, the road out of the quad was clearly marked. The job paid a good deal more than I was accustomed to earning, thereby encouraging me to be more openminded about the evils of business.

My first two post-collegiate jobs were with management-consulting firms doing a considerable amount of executive search. When I gained all the exposure necessary to develop my competence, and when my academic naïveté had been supplanted by a reasoned and experienced sense of purpose in what I was doing, I went out on my own. Within three years I had built up my practice to the point where I made an unusually good living. I feel good about that. More importantly, I feel good about having functioned well in more than one vocational role and that I am who I am, not because I work in the business world or because I left the world of scholarship. I try not to suffer fools gladly, and would be pleased to have you judge me by my friends, most of whom, by design, bear no relation to my business.

I like people as I imagine the Elizabethans or the Georgians liked them: faults and all, as long as they know what their motives are and aren't ashamed of them—even if I think their motives are questionable. My job is plainly a people job, and in that sense I am squarely in the right profession.

I recruit for all kinds of positions and I am not, therefore, restricted to meeting a certain category of executive; that would be boring. I am always looking for a person who will earn at least $20,000 a year, and more often than not the figure is markedly above that. Most of my clients are middle- or large-size corporations with large staffs. I typically search for executives who will run an entire division of a company or who will head the entire operation. I have served clients as disparate as large consumer packaged-goods companies and money managers, hotels and publishers, airlines and brewers. The only prerequisite for retaining me is that there be a corporate client who has a problem which he thinks can be solved by hiring the right executive. If he has faith that I understand his problems and if I have faith that he truly wants me to get him the best man for the job, I qualify for the assignment. Needless to say, my relationship to my corporate client is the cornerstone of my practice.

When I am dealing with first-rate clients who are honestly seeking to hire the best—the "superstars" of their industry—there is a tacit understanding that we will not waste our time on anything less than the best, and that we will have to pay dearly in salary and benefits. These "superstar" searches may be arduous, but at least they are aboveboard and fascinating, because the quality of the men with whom I'm dealing is excellent. It never fails, however, that when dealing with self-deluders, with second-rate managers looking to solve essential problems with superficial changes in management, I am bombarded with reminders that only the best executives will serve their needs. These men, afraid of the best because excellence poses a threat to their security, seldom have the candor to tell me that they want a competent journeyman, a good man who can keep things going as usual.

The hardest decision for a client to make is how candid he should be in dealing with a headhunter. Acting out of ignorance of the chief executive's real motives, a headhunter can be responsible for some terrible mistakes. Rapport is essential to a job well done.

By rapport, I don't mean mere cordiality and an easy flow of polite conversation. Rapport with a client means getting him to level with me and be honest about the company and the problems he faces in his department, or, if he is president, in the entire company.

By my definition, a business problem is not an indication of some fatal flaw in a company, but simply an obstacle which must be overcome to meet corporate objectives. If I can get a client to trust me with his most sensitive opinions, concerns and plans, I can be of more assistance than even he may be aware.

Many clients are embarrassed at their problems and try to hide them from me. That is like lying to a doctor about one's most telling symptoms. I will never betray a client's trust, but unpleasant truths must be shared with me if I am to do a superior job. Sometimes I have to remind a client that I have seen successful companies do silly things, and that I am not disgusted, embarrassed, or contemptuous of the foibles on his mind. I have come to regard irrationalities, vanities, and hyperbole as a corporate way of life. I enjoy them; it is comforting that high-and-mighty managements are as human as the rest of us.

Not only are clients sometimes embarrassed, they are also fragile. Many, upon using someone like me for the first time, feel it an admission of weakness. They have swallowed the bromide that if you are a well-managed company, you always have someone within the organization who can be entrusted with solving a chronic problem. These are the kinds of managements that hire a mailroom clerk when the president retires.

I remember reading a study in the *Journal of Religion and Health* which demonstrated the semiconscious hostility between divorce lawyers and their clients. The initial relationship headhunters have with new clients is somewhat like that. The companies need us, but they dislike the necessity.

Because clients sometimes feel this way, it is only natural that they not be completely cooperative and sometimes openly resentful of my probing questions. Knowing that clients are often ill at ease in working with me, it would be foolish for me to display my annoyance or frustration.

One might not be aware that the most harmful and common misunderstanding between client and headhunter involves the issue of *attracting* accomplished job candidates. When a client calls me in to do a search, he usually wants me to uncover executives who have reputations for outstanding accomplishment. They must have high intelligence, planning ability, leadership, "charisma," education, and be the right age. After hearing these predictable specifications outlined to me, I inform the client if I will be able to present two or three such individuals in sixty to ninety days. Ordinarily I can.

However, I tell a client that the candidates I'm going to present aren't "job seekers" and aren't "in the market" for another job and are going to have to be romanced somehow. My client will usually nod his head affirmatively and say, "Great—you bring 'em in and we'll take it from there."

For some reason, the meaning of this "non-job seeker" business rarely comes across to the client. Clients often are not prepared to deal with the "interviewee" who is not in the market. The client who begins a meeting where I have introduced such a candidate with the question, "Why do you want to make a change?" wrenches my innards.

An accomplished man making his maximum contribution to a company is basically a contented man. He is a person so talented that his company in truth would be hurting if they lost him. Because this is so, the exceptional man is usually well rewarded financially and emotionally. Consequently, for some time he has not considered making a job change. If you wanted this man on your management team, and knew that because of his experience and superior abilities he would reduce your corporate risk in a crucial area to the barest minimum if you had him, wouldn't you agree that getting him would pose a formidable challenge?

Precisely—but fewer than one in ten clients are prepared to face up to this and meet the challenge. As a result, I hold in abeyance the client's request for the best until I know he means it.

If a client actually wants one of the top three or four people in an industry, he simply has to pay a premium for the security of knowing that he, in fact, has one of the best. It most often requires of the client an unusually high compensation package, perhaps stock, and more autonomy than the candidate has in his present circumstances. A search for such a person cannot be undertaken with any hope for success if the client's corporate compensation structure is not ahead of the rest of his industry. If the client wants an exceptional man, he has to react in an exceptional way.

I won't argue with a client who consciously concludes he doesn't need a superstar to help solve a particular problem. His honesty enables me to draw up realistic specifications and present him with men of average talents whose career and compensation requirements won't fracture the pattern of the other executives in the company. As long as I'm made a party to the client's decision, and he hasn't smoke-screened me with big talk about his high standards, I can do a much better job of helping him. I can eliminate the wasted effort and embarrassment of presenting a man to do a boy's job.

However, if my client insists on deluding himself, and I am assured that I have done my best to dissuade him from so doing, my conscience is clear with regard to him. It is anything but clear, however, with regard to the man I must try to hire—the man who, in the argot of my profession, is termed the candidate.

When my client is a knowledgeable, no-nonsense business executive, with a corporate problem that demands outstanding, experienced personnel, my task can be technically difficult; I may have to interview numerous candidates; I may have to write hundreds of letters, ask for leads from all my contacts, run complicated and expensive computer programs, coordinate my findings with the impression my men make on my client, perhaps, even, travel throughout the world. These superstar searches test my mettle, but they never involve me in deceiving the candidate.

As I have said, if the candidate is the right man for the job, he is usually not in the job market. One of the biggest mistakes a candidate can make in an interview is to show me that he is hungry for the job I am describing. If I seem to be saying something as obvious as "Play hard-to-get so the recruiter will think your present employer loves you," that is only a small part of my advice. Candidates almost always forget a headhunter's first responsibility is to his corporate client, and it may be in the client's best interest not to hire you. The candidate whose strongest pitch is that he "really" wants the job is showing an inadequate sense of what the priorities of our meeting are all about. The cagey candidate will spend most of his time trying to find out what the client's problem is, giving the impression that understanding the corporate problem is his first concern. Only after this professional and cool-seeming examination of the objective reasons for the interview should a candidate even hint he might be interested. And if he has shown an astute understanding of the client's needs, his silence will usually draw the headhunter into becoming the suitor. In the executive-search business, it's a lot better to be pitched to than to be pitching.

Too few candidates realize that the headhunter may have sought them out for reasons quite apart from trying to find them a job. For example, he may be looking for an unattractive character to parade before his client so that another candidate may appear more attractive by contrast. He may be adding yet another name to his list because some of his clients think he is performing well only when he marches hordes of candidates, good and bad, before them. And, most subtly of all, he may want to produce for his client just the man he has specified, so when it comes to making the expensive decision to hire him, he will be forced at last into seeing he had overstated the human solution with which he would be content to live.

The only candidates who need fear these devices are those who would want a job for which they are either not qualified or in which they would not be happy. And such men are usually not the most skilled or personable. However, it is amusing to remember an exceptional case where the candidate wanted a job he knew he would dislike and for which he admitted he was overqualified. Not only did he make these admissions, but I recommended him for the $55,000-a-year post that he subsequently got.

In this particular case, the job required copywriting talent along with managerial know-how, and while the salary was high, the job involved tedious minutiae in connection with a tawdry line of products, and was surrounded by managers with whom my candidate would not get along. Were a man to have the right qualifications for the job, he would not, in all likelihood, have the stomach for it. I quickly figured that I would be filling a job likely to become, in a relatively short while, vacant—either because the candidate would become dissatisfied and look elsewhere or because my client would become dissatisfied with the half-hearted, grudgingly bestowed efforts of the new man.

The reason everything worked out perfectly for all concerned was that both client and candidate were out to screw each other. My client wanted top talent to iron out problems in his organization so that he could hire less expensive help to do the job made possible by his short-lived superstar. In short, I'm convinced that under some suitable guise he intended to fire the superstar the moment things were put back in working order. On the other side, my superstar wanted a quick bankroll and a prestigious step up the corporate ladder. He intended to start looking for another job the day he was hired. I had found the right fink for the right rat. I also collected my fee.

Let me return to my observation that it is the wise candidate who appears not to be in the job market. An intelligent man doing an excellent job should be content both with the quality of his chores and the amount of his remuneration. You and I know, however, that in an imperfect world virtue often goes unrewarded, and a perfectly splendid employee may be getting short shrift from management. But a candidate should never admit this, because in the Calvinistic world of the corporation the disparity between virtue and reward is less likely to be read as injustice than as just deserts.

It is essential, therefore, for a candidate to remember that an executive recruiter is more likely to be impressed by a candidate's curiosity about the job and the company that needs it filled than he is by the candidate's answers to questions about himself. If the recruiter asks why the candidate is interested in the job under discussion, the candidate should parry the question by asking why the recruiter is interested in him. The candidate should give the impression that the recruiter's first task is to convince him, the man for whom he is buying an overly expensive, mediocre lunch, that there is something worth the candidate's time to listen to, and only when the candidate is convinced that he has been brought into the confidence of the recruiter should he speak candidly about himself.

The candidate must not be reluctant to ask blunt and seemingly indelicate questions; after all, it is his career which is at stake, and he's the one who has to protect it. The recruiter can find another candidate more easily than he can find another client.

In a headhunter interview, valor is the better part of discretion. Here is a list of some of the boorish thrusts with which you ought to challenge headhunters like me.

1. If this job is so hot, how come your client had to hire an expensive executive recruitment firm to fill it?

2. Describe to me the character of your client, and what kind of man does it take to get along with him?

3. Why did the last guy get fired?

4. Does your client want excellence or something else?

5. How much are you offering? And, since it's not enough, how much will you raise your offer and spice it with benefits?

6. How did you get my name? If you got it from someone who knows me and whom I respect, I'm impressed. If you got it out of a computer run or through some corporate gossip, you'll obviously have to spend a lot of my valuable time verifying my quality.

7. How much do you know about the kind of work I do? If not a lot, how can you judge me?

8. How much does your opinion of me count with your client? If not a lot, when do I meet him?

9. Are you aware that if this conversation isn't kept confidential, I'll kill you?

The client would like the candidate to believe that job opportunities are in a seller's market; the candidate wants the client to believe his services are in a buyer's market. Smart parties on either side will maintain this ritual fiction;

my job is to mediate, satisfying all parties, and happily, by so doing, myself.

Experience has taught me that there is one kind of search that one should never undertake: the fruitless one, the search in which the client cannot be satisfied or in which the job up for grabs is beneath the dignity of the man he is demanding fill it. I can collect handsome per diem fees for these searches, but meanwhile frustrate myself, disappoint my candidates, give my client reason to be unhappy with me, and, lastly, not collect my percentage of the selected candidate's first year's salary. If, as Santayana has said, fanaticism consists of redoubling your efforts when you have lost sight of your aim, I try never to lose sight of mine, which is to run as profitable a practice as possible while satisfying to the fullest possible measure the wishes of my clients.

I have indicated the kind of psychological jousting in which the client, recruiter, and candidate become involved—the self-deception, pretension, subtle power-playing, all of which require of a corporate headhunter keen wits and a steady hand, a subtle, sometimes cynical and yet sanguine view of human frailty, and a strong sense of his own perspicacity and worth; for, in the trade I ply, it is not honesty and expertise and compassion which are most useful, but the appearance thereof. And it is the subtlety of this distinction between the apparent and the real which separates the boor in my profession from the *Mensch*. Because to prevaricate without recognizing the mode, and to do so without an ironic sense, is to take from one's successes the retributive share of melancholy which are their due.

I do not shy from the essentially materialistic, often hypocritical aspects of the executive-headhunting profession, but I want to make clear that as much as we corporate consultants initiate circumlocutious arcanities and the simulacra of expertise rather than its substance, we are forced into so doing by a business ethic that often can swallow nothing less familiar: the truth, for instance. I am honest and sensitive enough to prefer dealing with any business problem frankly and intelligently if I can do so without alienating my client. But more often than not, I've got to make compromises.

By now you have noticed that I use the term "headhunter" unabashedly to describe what it is I do to make a living. For reasons I don't fully understand, this word is anathema to my brethren in executive-search consulting. While the term may connote a lack of professionalism for some, I regard it as implied respect, much the same as qualified psychiatrists are referred to as "shrinks." At any rate, it is an accurate description of what we do: we hunt heads. And just how we headhunters go about doing that is the subject of the next section of this book.

II. THE HEADHUNTER

About the last place on earth you'd expect to hear revolutionary talk about the corporation is at the Wrigley Building's well-known bar in Chicago. On any working day the room is crowded with advertising and marketing types, still feeling the well-being of their three-martini lunches. Arms around one another's shoulders, they put on a display that owes as much to Dale Carnegie's dictum that it is ethical to form friendships for ulterior purposes as it does to barman Bob Turney's light touch with the vermouth.

On one occasion, I visited the bar with a friend who is public-relations director of a mammoth oil company. He was telling me about his efforts to promote Black-owned filling stations, which, he speculated, would not only accomplish a social good, but also protect the company against losses. After all, if you're going to burn down a business, you probably won't burn down the one you own. He was planning to address an American Management Association meeting and the title of his address was "Does the Publicly Owned

Corporation Have a Right to be Socially Responsible?'' In other words, can a corporation ethically act in a manner that reduces profit?

I nearly choked on my Old Bushmills. The assumption that the sole responsibility of ownership was to produce the maximum profit went out with Spencer's Social Darwinism and John D. Rockefeller's dime tips.

I told my companion that, as soon as he had delivered his speech, he might want to send his résumé to me, and that in five or ten years I was certain I'd be able to find something for him.

Somehow he managed to ignore my cleverness. Couldn't I see how such a zinger might be salutory? he inquired. ''Ask any businessman or corporate investor if he wants his company to be a force for good and he'll generously agree that he does. Ask the same man if he'll approve of corporate expenditures for socially responsible but financially risky ventures, and you'll probably find a liberal turned Scrooge. By making the business community aware of how difficult it is to escape from the solely pecuniary basis of its operations, might I not embarrass a few corporate departments out of their sanctimonious promotion fodder? I might even encourage the notion that if profit and social good don't coexist in the corporation, it might be time to start changing the corporation.''

There are few people in corporate life whose intelligence and character I admire more than this man's, and later that night, and for many days to follow, I pondered those remarks and others he made in the same vein. There was no way I could disagree with him, and that was why I felt so lousy. Yet I didn't think I could recommend him for a position I had been hired to fill, and for which our seemingly casual meeting was a disguised exploration.

This particular hunt was initiated by a large international farming and canning company beset with labor unrest and a corporate image of gigantism. They were looking for a combination lobbyist and public-information officer who would put the company's many years of substantial but little known social activism in the spotlight. The president who retained my firm was sincere in his belief that his company had made great social contributions and that it would continue to do so. He recognized the injustices being done to migrant labor and acknowledged the undue influence of some of America's corporations on the internal affairs of under-developed nations. He also knew that in corporations generally, few Blacks or Mexicans occupied managerial positions —something his company was an exception to in a small way. That's why he demanded from me "absolutely the best man in corporate public relations." And he was willing to pay through the nose.

I didn't doubt his sincerity. What I knew, however, was that his idea of what constituted significant and prompt social remedies was conservative. I also knew that his Board of Directors were about as receptive to change as the bron-tosaurus, and that the stock of the company had plateaued for five years. What was needed here was a shrewd corporate infighter—a man who could camouflage his ethical zeal behind a facade of business as usual. My oil-company man was not that type. His eloquence, his directness, his impa-tience would make his star burn brightly, but only for a short time.

My colleagues in the executive-recruitment business can be divided into two classes: salesmen and professionals. Both are out to collect fees. Where they differ is that the salesman is trying to come up with a candidate he thinks the client can be *persuaded to buy,* while the professional is trying to come up with a candidate he *believes will do the job.* Both ask to get paid.

Invariably, the client who is flabbergasted by what we

headhunters ask to be paid has never used us before. Perhaps that only proves that after you've been hit on the head enough you don't notice the pain. Another theory is that until you see how valuable we can be you can't understand why my fees begin at $250 a day, plus all expenses. I also get 25 percent of the candidate's first year's compensation. That means that if I place a man in a $50,000 a year job, I take $12,500 home to the bank. In one year one of my best corporate clients paid me $60,000 in fees. In a good year a senior partner in a major headhunting firm makes about $100,000. The average non-partner recruiter will make $20,000 to $30,000. There is always the possibility that I will not come up with the right man, and my client will then be out the $250 per diem. And yet, my fees have never once been questioned by a client who has used me at least twice. I must be doing something right. But I can't do anything right, however, unless I understand clearly what the client wants.

The eternal predicament of the professional headhunter is that what the client wants is often not what he needs. Most likely a salesman would have recruited my socially minded friend for the canning company and wound up with a frustrated candidate and a disappointed client. Even the sweet taste of the hefty fee might also turn sour, particularly if the client were to convey his ill feelings to his friends in potential client companies, thereby depriving me of a crack at some long-range quality business.

On the other hand, I am sorry to say that in many instances there is no substantial difference between the job done by a salesman and a professional. One of the persistent frustrations of my business is that many of the executive searches I'm hired to perform do not allow for the exercise of my professional talents. When I'm caught up in one of these corporate fox-trots, there can be no difference between apparent and real virtues.

One kind of assignment that allows of little professionalism is the one in which the only course of action is to do nothing at all, but to do it with a flourish.

A nationally known advertising agency noted for the genius of its creativity inherited a major toothpaste account, which had been with another agency for over ten years. The product was a perennial best seller, but until recently, like Hershey bars, had not been given extensive mass-advertising exposure. In recent years, sales, which neither time nor tide had ever seemed to affect, had slumped. Its package was ugly; the print on the carton couldn't have been read by a person with the visual acuity of a young Ted Williams; the product tasted like scouring powder and smelled like an operating room. It was notably lacking any miracle ingredient approved by the American Dental Association.

The agency devised a high-powered campaign. First, they recommended a change in the formulation of the toothpaste. Second, they redesigned the package: Third, they tried to introduce some glamour into the graphics. The client rejected all these suggestions, and accordingly, sales continued to slump. It was time for a new agency to rupture themselves in the Sisyphian task of moving the product upward. It was also at that point that I was brought in.

The company executive who interviewed me wore pleated trousers and black oxfords, like my father used for church. He did not have on a button-down collar, as one might expect, but a rumpled white broadcloth shirt which had long ago lost its collar stays and was frayed at the gray cuffs. He had a face out of Grant Wood, and when he spoke, he exposed his upper teeth like Don Adams used to do on *Get Smart*. It didn't take me long to figure out two essentials. One, everything the advertising agency had suggested was as appropriate as it was unacceptable. And, two, the most devout desire of the company brass was to be left alone so they could continue doing business as they always had. I was continually told that the firm wanted someone who was "loyal," someone who "appreciated what had been accomplished in the past," someone who knew the importance of "continuity." In short, this company was begging to be told there was no need to tell it anything. My task was to find a corporate advertising manager who would do just that.

You just may think that it's difficult to find a genius. But it doesn't compare with the difficulty of finding the perfect dullard. I must admit that I'd had little experience with separating the chaff from the wheat. But the story has a happy ending. We found a middle-aged fundamentalist who lived with his mother, shied away from fried foods, wore gray clocking on his hose, and probably got into advertising because of his passion for double-entry bookkeeping. Most remarkably, he also brushed his teeth with the client's product. His name was given me by a copywriter whom he'd fired for having an affair with his secretary. Of this man's personality it can be truly said that when he entered a room it was as if someone had just left. I earned my fee and would have felt justified in billing the client twice as much.

Doing nothing with a flourish is one of the most common of the bogus consultantships I am required to perform. But it's nowhere as embarrassing as another kind of assignment in which my client has already made up his mind about how to handle his problem and hires me to mouth his conclusions. Often he may lack the confidence necessary to proceed alone and is subconsciously demanding affirmation from an outside source. More shrewdly, he may have thought long and hard about his problem and done intricate research about how to implement his conclusions. The reason he hires me is to get "independent" corroboration which he can then use to pressure through suggestions he himself has already made.

On this kind of mission it's just as embarrassing when your client's conclusions are wrong as when they're right. If he's wrong, you sell yourself cheap by mouthing the pseudosolutions he's feeding you. If he's right, you're accepting a fee for allowing your client to do all your work—something like a surgeon's being paid for allowing the patient to perform the appendectomy. I try not to get involved in this kind of assignment, but usually, by the time I find out that I'm being used, I've done enough work so that not collecting my fee would be masochistically scrupulous.

A medium-size book-publishing company, which had grown out of a successful educational magazine, was finding that its book division was growing less profitable on expanding volume. I was hired ostensibly to help find the reasons why and, if necessary, to recruit the proper executive to overcome this problem.

The company was typical of the book business in that its editor in chief enjoyed considerable prestige, attracted most of the literary properties the firm acquired, performed or delegated most of the day-to-day work of his division, and yet had very little authority with the slide-rule boys, money managers, and market analysts at the corporate level. The editor's taste was sacrosanct as long as the financial people agreed with it, and the business boys obviously were qualified to make literary judgments because they had learned to spell "dollar" in college. The senior executives were breathing down the editor in chief's neck to increase profits. Whenever he made a cut in the operating expenses of his own department, he was applauded. Whenever he suggested that more money needed to be spent in other departments to support his department's efforts, he was ignored. Finally he hit on a plan he thought the slide rules would understand. He wanted a company management-organization study to be conducted by me and a market analysis, prepared by someone else, of the kinds of books which sold best in certain markets. The slide rules bought his plan and I was called in.

I spent several days with the editor in chief, during which

time he convinced me that virtually no statistical analysis could reveal whether or not a work of fiction would sell or collect dust. He showed me that it was almost impossible to foretell if space advertising would move a book. He demonstrated conclusively that the job of an editor couldn't be submitted to input-output studies, and he predicted correctly that the market-research firm that had been retained would discover the same thing. In short, I concluded I was wasting my time talking to him—which, of course, was exactly what he wanted me to conclude. He suggested that I drop in to chat with the advertising and promotion department. I complied.

It took me approximately one-half day to see how hopelessly undermanned and overworked this department was. In the vast rush of books that arrived on their desks every week, they could properly attend only to obvious winners in the marketplace. The morale of the staff was low because there was no way for them to do their jobs well. Their advertising budget was set up at the beginning of the fiscal year. Consequently, a good book placed unexpectedly on the publishing list toward the end of the budget period could not be given proper advertising and promotion. This caused the editors to yell at the advertising and promotion department and the advertising and promotion department to sneer at the naiveté of the editors. In short, I had found the bottleneck.

I went back to the editor in chief. I told him what I had concluded. He handed me a twenty-page memo, complete with charts, which reorganized the advertising and promotion department so that each editor became an account executive for his own titles, with advertising and promotion people reporting to him. The budget was to be determined by the editor in chief. When I asked him how he had done so much work since our last talk, he told me he was a fast typist.

In due time I submitted a report to top management, which, in substance, was much like the editor in chief's brainchild.

Because in this case the company was more prepared to listen to me than to him, my recommendations carried more weight than his would have. Shrewd man. He got what he wanted and I must admit that I agreed with his assessment of the organizational problem. But that assignment still leaves a bad taste in my mouth.

If the president of a well-established mutual fund company hadn't been as amused by his own strategy as I was bewildered by it, I would have considered my consulting job for him one of the most useless I had ever allowed myself to become embroiled in, no matter how unwittingly. The fund had grown so large that it had lost much of its ability to get in and out of the market with enough securities to affect significantly the value of its shares. In fact, it had become almost as difficult to make a mistake as it was to buy or sell wisely. The fund, by virtue of its diversity, gyroscopically balanced itself.

The president called me in to help him think through an idea involving a network of financial, political, and corporate experts who would report to the fund in the form of an exclusive newsletter conveyed either in print or by some electronic medium. My client was a reticent, inarticulate man who made investment decisions with the mysterious suddenness of St. Paul being visited by the Holy Spirit on the road to Damascus. And like a religious mystic, he was held in awe by some people. Others found his credentials questionable. He had surrounded himself with a battery of hard-working financial, legal, governmental, and economic experts, all of whom bid for his attention like lovesick troubadours in an Italian romance. One morning, while we were discussing his new idea, he asked me to sit in on a high-level discussion to be held the following day. At this meeting certain changes in the policy of the International Monetary Fund would be evaluated in terms of the effect they would have on particular securities in which the mutual fund had strong positions.

I told him I didn't know much about the securities in question and was totally unschooled about the IMF. Later that afternoon my client's secretary called me and asked me to meet him at his private club. I was given no further information. When I arrived, I was greeted not only by him but by his top assistant, who was known for his mastery of economics and an uncanny sense of what does and does not happen in the stock market. For two hours the assistant told me all he could about IMF and about the securities which were the subject of the next day's meeting. When our meeting broke up and the assistant was sent back to the office, the client asked me what I thought. I said I was immeasurably impressed. He said that I shouldn't be, that most of what the assistant told me was a crock. He disappeared into the dusk.

Next morning at 10 A.M. we gathered in the client's office for the important meeting. The two senior vice-presidents for investment were there, as was the corporation counsel. The first senior vice-president, who was a technical analyst, referred to expensively produced charts and graphs to which his junior associate pointed in perfect coordination with the points his boss was making. He concluded after about half an hour that the fund should not buy the 150,000 shares of corporation X which had been suggested. "Sounds good," said my client. Then it was senior vice-president Number 2's turn.

He didn't put much faith in the technical indexes that had so absorbed senior vice-president Number 1's time. What was important in his opinion was to know the products corporation X was making; to be familiar with the people who managed the company; to understand the historic trends in company X's field. His presentation was a model of historical detail, a perfect portrait that humanized the company and made its activities seem more than just cold numbers. He concluded that corporation X was sound, that the fund should immediately take a strong position and buy in again if the stock showed a short-term drop in market value. "Well, that sounds good also," said my client, who thanked the men for their reports and dismissed the meeting. I remained behind.

"What did you think of the reports?" the client asked. I said I thought they were brilliant, and I didn't see how they could be improved upon by any number of additional men he might have reporting from the field.

"Yes, I see your point," he said, "but the reason I want you to come up with a cadre of reporters exposed to a wide spectrum is so these guys will think I haven't learned enough from them."

"I can understand that," I said, "but isn't it too expensive to hire top men to report to you when you really don't need the information they're reporting?"

"What makes you think I don't need the information?" he said. "I'm making investment decisions in which millions of dollars are involved, and if it looks as if I'm not spending a lot of money to make sure I'm right, the justification for this entire fund goes down the drain."

"But what are you going to tell those two guys who just left here?"

"I'm going to tell them I've hired you to recruit the analysts for our new intelligence-gathering network, which will report directly to them. That way they'll wonder whether or not I thought their presentations knowledgeable, and at the same time they'll think I admire them enough to want to give them all the help I can."

"But what are you going to do about buying or selling the company they were talking about?"

"I'm going to buy 10,000 shares and let them both wonder. Then I'm going to buy 100,000 shares of Xerox."

"Why Xerox?"

"I've just got this hunch. . . ."

No management consultant who has pride in his work knowingly becomes involved in nonsense such as this. Nonetheless, I wish I were able to summon more indignation with which to denigrate my colleagues who consider landing such assignments ripe plums rather than poison apples. I find I cannot. When there's a lot of money to be made for very little effort and when the client's gratitude is in direct proportion to the flimsiness of the hoax he has asked us to perpetrate, indignation comes hard.

When I come off a bogus assignment or hear about one in which a fellow headhunter has become involved, my thoughts turn not so much on the venality and banality of such dealings, but on what it is that justifies me in thinking *myself* different.

There can be no professionalism in my business without a highly developed knowledge of corporate life. The phony management consultant who pitches a bill of goods because he's ignorant and incompetent doesn't annoy me as much as some of my beautifully educated, highly intelligent, deeply experienced colleagues who too often set out to sell iceboxes to Eskimos. The only guarantee of professionalism in my business is something in addition to technical competence. It is an attitude.

I think of myself as a professional because for me there is no more fulfilling experience than to work in intelligent and amiable tandem with a client; to agree with, share, work toward, and, in some cases, help formulate his corporate objectives. To have established with my client a bond of trust *based on my competence* is the reward I prize most highly. Without this attitude I think it is next to impossible to maintain high professional standards over the long haul.

The temptations not to do so are too great.

The reward that most obviously competes with knowledge of the job well done is making money, and without clients who are willing to retain you, you're not going to make much money. All headhunters become skilled in pleasing clients. The difference between the salesman and the professional is that the salesman will be selling cosmetic virtues which may or may not have anything to do with his client's needs, while the professional always addresses himself to his client's real or imagined problem.

One of the cleverest phonies I ever knew specialized in recruiting candidates for clients with social pretensions. He became quite a virtuoso. This headhunter—let us call him Chip Fairfax—could trace his ancestry back to Noah (who he would have insisted was Episcopalian) and had committed the social register of each important United States city to memory. He spent the year going through the annual reports of the *Fortune 500* and compiling a list of the most influential executives at those corporations who were members of the right clubs and who would most likely be impressed by Chip's social credentials.

If Chicago was his target area, he'd pick out some silver-spooned, nasal-toned (in Manhattan they call it "honking") stuffed shirt and find out to which clubs he belonged, such as Onwentsia, Barrington Hills or The Oak Brook Polo Club. One could be certain that Chip was either a member or had friends who were, and he made a point of belonging to several clubs which had reciprocal privileges. He had a way of being where he needed to be.

Chip would show up when his quarry was expected. This intelligence could easily be obtained from club employees, from clubmates, and by just keeping up with several club social calendars. After engaging his "catch" in conversation, Chip would let a week pass and then send a letter:

DEAR TOWNLEY:

It was sure great bumping into you and Buffy at the Club. Next time remind me not to play tennis with you *after* the G and T's. But actually, I enjoyed meeting you and the Missus, and I hope if you're ever down Chevy Chase way in April you'll use our pad there for Hunt Cup.

I ran into a friend of yours at "The Knick" the other day, Forsyth Vanderkellen. Says you had a great passage during the Newport-Bermuda thing. Calls you quite a gob. At any rate, Vandy told me there are some things going on at International Electron that really drive him up the wall. I thought it would be nice were you to keep him in mind. It seems his wife, Martha, and your Buffy played field hockey at Miss Porter's. Can you believe it?

I'm enclosing his résumé. Let's keep in touch. And remember Hunt Cup.

It might actually be that Vanderkellen isn't looking for a job and that Chip is simply fishing. Since any interest in Vanderkellen would be channelled through Chip's firm, Vanderkellen needn't ever find out that Chip is using their friendship as a commodity to churn business. Chip has no notion whatever of the kind of job Townley may need filled. He's just hoping that Townley's snobbery can be counted on to turn Townley's attention to Chip's firm whenever a search assignment becomes necessary. Townley knows nothing about Vanderkellen's capacities or interests and has had no opportunity to find out if Chip is a good judge of corporate talent or of managerial problems. In fact, Vanderkellen may wind up having nothing to do with the business Chip and Townley may have between them.

Although social snobbery, good looks, the right dress and

manner of speech are the most obvious kinds of cosmetic come-ons, they are by no means the most insidious. The average manager may be favorably disposed toward them, but, in the long run, he's got a problem to solve which if handled incorrectly could cost him his job. He is not likely, therefore, to be dazzled by gloss alone.

The history of success which a management-consulting firm can honestly list is an important sales asset, but let the corporate client beware when a headhunter's pitch is centered on what his company has done elsewhere.

By the time a corporate client has invited a headhunter into his confidence, he has made a preliminary determination (right or wrong) that the firm he represents is honorable and competent. What will most impress the corporate client is the headhunter's questions and/or observations about the specific problems of his client, not implicitly boastful references to his past triumphs. The effect of such self-puffing may be to imply that the headhunter finds it difficult to think of the problem at hand in any terms other than those he has already faced. The other drawback of puffing is psychological. The client should not believe that the headhunter is *trying to sell* his services. The sell should begin only after the headhunter has been given a chance to understand the problem at hand. Theoretically, there might be a corporate problem which the headhunter would not want to work on; he can't know this until he's heard his client out.

For example, his client might be a family-owned business which is having difficulties in keeping its top executives because the corporation refuses to offer stock options. The corporation may need top personnel for highly skilled and sensitive tasks. Headhunters often would not recommend their best candidates for such a job.

Again, a corporate vice-president of marketing may have

discovered that his sales force is not keeping up with the competition, and what he wants is a vigorous, imaginative sales manager who will initiate a hiring plan that will phase out "dead wood." Upon inspection of the company, the headhunter discovers that the reason the company's sales force has become uncompetitive is that the president has a penchant for overinvesting in manufacturing equipment without the proportionate return in productivity. The product the salesmen "buy" from their own corporation is priced sky-high and they cannot get the margins they need for their commissions or bonuses to be attractive. The headhunter reports this to the vice-president who called him in for the assignment and is told this is the way the president wants to do things and there's nothing to be done about it. Any headhunter who took on the job of helping to reorganize the sales force would be in for a difficult, if not impossible, challenge.

Before a headhunter offers his services he should find out if the corporate executive who is charged with retaining him has the authority to implement the cure the headhunter may suggest. I know of a headhunter who told the divisional manager of a pharmaceuticals company that the only way to increase the sales of his proprietary drug was to redesign the package and change his system of distribution. This advice came at a time when there was several months' inventory in retail stores with an equal amount in the warehouse. The client had asked for a suggestion that would reflect in the next quarter's balance sheet. The headhunter could not offer such a miracle.

The headhunter who tries to snow his corporate client with a recital of his credits is risking more than being thought a braggart. The first job of a headhunter is to listen. The shrewd corporate client wants most of all to know what you can do for him. He considers his own problems unique, and he doesn't like to hear about their commonality. In most instances the client will base his decision on whether or not to hire me on his impression of just how hard I've listened to his own specific problems. He knows that the headhunter who will take on any assignment is more concerned with churning business than solving problems.

One of the most amusing put-downs delivered by a corporate manager to a self-styled management expert is told in Edward Engberg's perceptive and witty book, *Spy in the Corporate Structure*,[1] about Alfred Bloomingdale, the founder and president of the prestigious and successful Bloomingdale's department store in New York City. A management expert was trying hard to convince Mr. Bloomingdale that his system of accounting was terribly outmoded and would eventually cause serious cash-flow problems. The venerable Mr. Bloomingdale took the energetic young consultant by the elbow and led him to Bloomingdale's tiny office in which was a wooden pushcart with which Mr. Bloomingdale had made his living during his first years in the New World.

"Do you see that pushcart?" said Mr. Bloomingdale.

"Yessir," said the young consultant.

"Then look around you," said Bloomingdale, gesturing expansively toward the entire department store. "All the rest is profit."

The dangers of clogged ears and gushing mouth I have spoken of; and while these faults may result in misunderstanding that can ruin a consulting relationship, there are dangers arising not from ignorance but from knowledge, and these can be equally harmful to a relationship if not served up in sweet enough recipes.

Quite often, after talking with a client for just a short while, I can see that he isn't leveling with me, and I know that

[1] Edward Engberg, *Spy in the Corporate Structure*. New York: World, 1967.

unless I get the true picture of what is happening inside his company I'm not going to be able to do my job adequately. I divide the executives who aren't leveling with me into two categories: those running scared and those running malicious. The scared type usually wins my sympathy if not my cooperation. One such executive, who was the division general manager of a corporation where I was doing an organization study, dictated the following memo to his secretary:

> Al Cox, the management consultant whom you met yesterday, will be back Tuesday, September 21 at 10 A.M. He will want to talk with some of our people. Please assist him in scheduling etc. He will use my office for his interviews as I will be on the West Coast next week.
> Please set up the following people and take care of scheduling, notifying, etc.

Tues. 9/21
   10:00 Santorini
   12:00 Lunch with Daley
   2:00 Smith
   4:00 Morris

Wed. 9/22
   9:00 Stensbrud
   11:00 Frederick
   1:00 Carson

> This schedule will probably not be adhered to exactly, but this will be a start. Be sure no one forgets.
>
> STAN
>
> P.S. In case someone looks concerned when you schedule him, please assure them Al Cox doesn't bite—I'm still alive—Ha! Ha!

A malicious client who comes immediately to mind is the

president of a supermarket chain headquartered in one of the major cities in the Midwest. The company was started, like many grocery chains, as a mom-and-pop store on the corner. The man's mother and father had started the pioneer store over thirty years ago and had made enough money at it to feed, clothe, and educate four sons, all of whom grew up with the business and who are still active in its management.

The parents passed away, but our client, being the eldest and most driven of the brothers, assumed the leadership of the company and set it on its course for growth. The company did well. I was called in to do a brief management survey and search. The chain was doing just under $100 million sales annually after years of plugging along at a $10 to $15 million sales level. In the four or five years prior to my becoming involved with them as a consultant, the organization had been multiplying sales by opening new retail outlets.

When I made arrangements with our client, Max, I told him I wanted to undertake a one- or two-day survey and interview his key managers. "I like to do this," I told him, "because I get a feel for the pace and spirit of the company. I also learn a bit about your business, the way you do things, what you value and what you don't. It also gives me a chance to feel at first hand the problem you are experiencing. Hopefully, we can overcome it by realigning your management team or bringing in a talented person from the outside." What I did not tell him is that I insist on these interviews because I can then determine better if this is a company that might use me repeatedly rather than for just this assignment; and, as capricious as it may sound, if I simply "like" them. One does not have to "like" a client and his people to do a good job, but as in the ad for the "Yellow Pages," it makes life a little easier.

Max reluctantly agreed to the survey prior to the search. Being a most authoritarian type, he did not like the thought of an interloper like me in his ranks, perhaps learning of problems he had not permitted himself to know.

After I interviewed his key people, three of whom were his younger brothers, I was prepared to meet with Max and make my recommendations. Ostensibly I had been brought in because Max and his brothers thought the financial control and reporting systems were in disarray. They thought they could straighten things out by directing me to find a hot-shot controller.

When I presented my observations to Max, some of which were fairly critical, they were met with only slight bristling. I had the feeling things were going well. I assumed he was pleased because I concurred with him and his brothers that they did, in fact, need a new controller. The present controller was one of the two non-brothers I interviewed, and I considered him woefully inadequate to his tasks. Max also seemed friendlier as the meeting wore on and he actually began to be expansive and tell me "confidential" plans for the company which was intelligence beyond what I would need to do my job. He volunteered that it would be a real help to me in my search for a corporate controller were the new man to know that the company would be taken "public" within two years, and that could only mean good things in the way of stock options. We parted on good terms, and I was left with the charge to unearth a top-quality vice-president-controller.

It was not until after presenting two first-rate candidates who were rejected for flimsy reasons that I began to suspect I was being ignored by Max. He often did not take my phone calls and wouldn't return them. Finally he derogated my expertise in a grudgingly granted phone call and canceled the assignment, which was now two months old.

From a source inside the company, I learned he was greatly offended by my observations. He considered every criticism I put forth a personal attack on his management effectiveness.

He was merely stringing me along. In the remote event that I came up with a candidate who met his fancy he would try to hire him at a salary considerably beneath what he said he was willing to pay. Max still has the same controller. The company has not "gone public" in the intervening years. He never paid my fee for time expended. The last I heard, he was having unusual difficulty getting suppliers. He is still running a sizable company like a mom-and-pop store.

If corporate managers often run scared it is not difficult to understand why. The value of most managers to their corporation is based on experience in that particular company and is often not marketable at equivalent levels with other corporations. One of the basic reasons for the hostility of "company types" to professionals is the well-founded suspicion that "a technical colleague is likely to have more in common with his counterpart in another company or on some college campus than with his non-professional associates."[2] His "disloyalty" has a basis in fact, because the professional carries with him the value he adds to the company which chooses to avail itself of his skills.

Another worry that the corporate manager may have is that "the economic justification of corporate luxury has never been seriously examined, and one may rightfully wonder if the thick pile on the floor, the rosewood desk, the new limousine, the first-class air travel are just ways of having a hand in the till while keeping custody of other people's money."[3]

Because the justification of their authority rests on a skill or art which has somehow escaped notice by most of us,

[2] Wilbert E. Moore, *The Conduct of the Corporation*. New York: Random House, 1962.
[3] *Ibid.*, p. 102.

many corporate managers spend much of their lives creating the simulacra of professionalism through pettifogging adherence to senseless procedure; or they may make extensive use of psuedoprofessional jargon in which readily understandable information is kept from common currency by pretending that it is knowledge accessible only to experts. The headhunter who doesn't understand the games that scared executives play will be so bewildered or so put off by his client's ritual self-justifications that he will lose lucrative assignments in which, once the bull-level is penetrated, he can render valuable service.

I've been told by advertising managers that the reason they weren't giving support to a product was because they couldn't come up with the right "mix," when what they meant was that they were badly over budget. I've heard publishers speak about "corporate break-even" figures as opposed to "author earn-out," when what they were really trying to do was justify cutting down further on advances paid to authors. I've heard managers of recently acquired heavy-machinery companies speak about the "synergistic" benefits of unified accounting and purchasing when what they were really trying to hide was their chagrin at having been taken over by a conglomerate. I've heard breakfast-food companies speak about capturing the "organic market," when what they meant was advertising to it rather than creating a product for it. And most recently I was thanked by a direct-mail specialist for the advice I had given him. He turned to me and with utter sincerity said, "Al, I want to thank you for your *input*."

A headhunter mustn't be taken in by this jargonized image of what a corporation and its managers are trying to do. He's got to be able to translate the tribal jargon into understandable truths and to realize that the poverty of corporate rhetoric is often a sign of intellectual exhaustion or an attempt to spruce up the banal. Arthur M. Schlesinger, Jr., captures the mode as well as anyone when he writes about the maddening lingo of the State Department:

> In meetings the men from State would talk in a bureaucratic patois borrowed in large part from the Department of Defense. We would be exhorted to "zero in" on "the purpose of the drill" (or of the "exercise" or "operation"), to "crank in" this and "phase out" that and "gin up" something else, to "pinpoint" a "viable" policy and, behind it, a "fall back position," to ignore the "flak" from competing government bureaus or from the communists, to refrain from "nit-picking" and never to be "counter-productive." Once we were "seized of the problem," preferably in as "hard-nosed" a manner as possible, we would review "options," discuss "overall" objectives, seek "breakthroughs," consider "crash programs," staff our "policies"—doing all these things preferably "meaningfully" and "in depth" until we were ready to "finalize" our deliberations, "sign on to" or "sign off on" conclusions (I never could discover the distinction, if any, between these two locutions) and "implement" a decision. This was not just shorthand; part of the conference-table vocabulary involved a studied multiplication of words. Thus one never talked about a "paper" but always a "piece of paper," never said "at this time" but "at this point in time."[4]

An investment advisor once told me, "If our economic model is on target, we feel earnings will be *trending* upwards." What I wanted to know was how an economic model aims at a target? Isn't the design of the model fashioned on what the corporation's targets are? And if so, isn't it a self-

[4] Arthur M. Schlesinger, Jr., *The Thousand Days*. New York: Houghton Mifflin Co., 1965, p. 417.

fulfilling prophecy to say that the model will hit the target?

The controller for a gas turbine manufacturer in the Midwest told me that his firm had "not yet shown a significant reversal of the overall pattern of accumulation." Was I supposed to be wiser?

And just so you don't think that headhunters are guiltless of verbal effluence, here are some selections from some of my earlier brochures. In one I promised my prospective clients that I would discuss the "specific nature of their operating problem." Leave out "nature" and "operating" and you begin to get a clear sentence. Big deal! I would discuss the "specific problem." Try to imagine my not doing so if asked.

In another I promised that after understanding what kind of candidate a client was searching for I would "write up and clearly delineate the Man Specifications." Have you ever wondered what *your* "Man Specifications" are? And how does your mental image change when I ask what are *her* "Woman Specifications"? And isn't it true that what I was really saying was that after talking with the client I would try to find the right man for the job?

Finally, in my profession we don't have "problems" but "problem situations." We never appraise something without "objectively" appraising it, and we never see anything but that it is "realistically perceived," so that it can be "explicitly recognized." Our search procedures are not only disciplined but also "directed" and "controlled." Just try to imagine a disciplined search that wasn't directed and controlled!

Corporations not only play tricks with words; as often, and with more harmful effect, they camouflage the real meaning of their attitude toward personnel. Most people who are even remotely familiar with the corporation know about the phenomenon called "being kicked upstairs." This procedure is less common, however, than its more waste-producing cousin, "being kicked across divisions." The cross-kick occurs most frequently when the product which an executive has been handling is either phased out of a company's operations or when the manager has done, up until now, a good job of running his division, but for some reason is no longer needed. The man has developed years of service and some justly earned prestige. The only problem is that there's nothing left for him to do, and no one thinks it fair to fire him. Thus the efficiency drive which led corporate-level management to discover his superfluity is directly squandered by discovering for him a superfluous position with another division. The manager who has been cross-kicked usually knows it, and, if he doesn't quit, acquiesces in his sinecure. Because he can't admit he has been given a sinecure, he begins to create the trappings of importance: He calls meetings; he writes endless memos; he commissions research studies in areas that don't need research; he haggles about promptness; he organizes the company charity drive; he fires people for slovenly dress; he mixes drinks at the boss's birthday party.

If a corporate headhunter is not going to be driven crazy by running errands for such a time-waster, he's got to be quick to recognize his mode, because the cross-kicked sinecurist often ends up running malicious, and is the instigator of the pointless executive search.

One of the favorite complaints of the malicious, cross-kicked client is that there is dissension in the ranks and that he feels some people are not living by the rules of the corporation. The manager may cite the usual virtuous platitudes of corporate conduct, but soon he will get down to specifics such as these I heard on one occasion.

"In Smith's division the number of invoices required by company policy are rarely if ever submitted. Receipted bills and claims for reimbursements for expenses in the line of duty are irregularly submitted and despite repeated warnings are sloppily executed and sometimes almost illegible. There are numerous, documented cases of Smith's men coming in late, and last week one of his men had alcohol on his breath when he visited an important customer. And, most important of all, there have been reports from all over the company and from many customers that Smith and his men are constantly abrasive.''

I was then told that Smith is a brilliant manager, filled with ideas and energy, but that for his own good he has to learn the meaning of teamwork.

One of the first lessons a headhunter learns is ''Beware the ass-kisser,'' and the surest sign of a gluteal osculator is the manager who elevates the amenities of corporate conduct to the level of a serious problem. The only indictment made by the cross-kicked sinecurist that I thought serious enough to investigate was the charge that Smith was abrasive.

Nurtured by what is frequently called the human-relations school, a popular business philosophy militates against the abrasive personality as suitable for management positions. It is reasoned that the abrasive person causes dissension, hostility, and ill-will among his management colleagues, all of whom must function in a coordinated fashion.

The essence of managerial function is coordination. The splicing of managerial skill with creative insight is rare. And if a subordinate has it, he is in danger, most often, from the charge of abrasiveness. Often abrasiveness is the result of extraordinary ability being frustrated in expression. Often it is the result of an inspired executive who is truly expert in a given area refusing to compromise achievement to get along with colleagues whose standards may be mediocre and whose motivation is questionable. Often it is merely the result of simple honesty, when a bright, judicious, perceptive person shoots holes in a business plan espoused by another member of management. Often it is the wake of the creative, aggressive person who wants to get something done and the red tape be damned.

The best place to air dirty linen is with the person who is allegedly responsible for the soiling. I went to Smith and asked him about his men's drinking and about their offensive breath. He said the only rule he'd laid down about drinking was that his men weren't to touch vodka. "I'd rather have the customer think my men were drunk than stupid." When I questioned him about expense accounts, he laughed and said the only thing worse than being fired for spending too much was spending too little. When he learned from me who had retained me as a consultant, he said, "I am blessed that I am known by my enemies." It wasn't hard to see that Smith wasn't going to play ball. Secretly, I was delighted at his sarcasm and sense of humor. Dealing with a man who was as self-assured as Smith in this delicate situation was a relief.

I asked Smith if I could interview his subordinates and he gave me a quick OK. They loved him. I find it peculiar that the executive labeled "abrasive" by some of his colleagues and considered harmful to morale often is precisely the one who has the highest morale among the men with whom he works.

The gifted, customarily outspoken, highly dedicated manager heartens his subordinates with his own superior performance. He inspires them with intelligence, drive, judgment, involvement, insight, and expertise. In the large bureaucratic corporation where "diplomacy" is revered, plain competence is sometimes a novel commodity. The saddest thing about competence is that sometimes it is not a noticeable benefit to the company.

More people are familiar with the concept of "malfeasance," doing the wrong thing, than they are with "misfeasance," doing the right thing the wrong way. Often, in order to do a job well, the creative manager must institute *ad hoc* procedures that obliterate traditional jurisdictional prerogatives or intrude personality into decisions that ought to be decided according to purely quantifiable data.

For example, a manager may have such loyalty to his company and such a distaste for the way its operations are being bollixed that he will take his insights directly to the top without touching base with his superiors in the hierarchical ladder of department heads and vice-presidents. The manager's justification for his leaping over jurisdictions may be that it is the jurisdictional setup which is itself the cause for the snafu.

A tightly knit division (Gimex) of a large pharmaceuticals company (Spectrum) was famous for the brilliance of its research and development department. In fact, since Spectrum's acquisition of Gimex, the profitability of Spectrum's complex and various ventures was largely due to huge yearly profits generated by a Gimex-discovered series of what were considered miracle drugs. In the stock market and economic woes of 1969–1970, Spectrum profits declined, and one nationally famous business journalist reported in his popular newsletter what many people within Spectrum were already saying: that Gimex hadn't come up with a profit-generating discovery since 1965 and was finding it harder to justify its budget—one of the largest in the drug industry. Then, in what appeared to be a crass disregard of his co-workers, the newly appointed Gimex president was quoted in a national weekly business magazine to the effect that Gimex had better come out of its ivory tower because it wasn't going to be possible for the division to rest on its laurels as it might have done under previous administrations.

The Gimex president began to institute austerity measures. Travel and entertainment budgets were slashed. R & D expenditures were likewise curtailed, and all the usual cost-cutting measures were implemented. Working at home was banned, and, probably most annoyingly to the technical people, each scientist at Gimex was to take a one-month, three-session-per-week orientation course so that he might better understand the other operations of Spectrum. Then, as a direct slap in the face of the scientists, the divisional sales manager was made a vice-president.

The effect on morale was immediate and danger of mass resignation was real. One of my previously placed executives was the youngest of the Gimex vice-presidents. He held a meeting with the president in which he as a representative of the staff placed its complaints on the table. He pointed out that it was a maxim of the business that there was a minimum lag of at least five years, usually longer, between the discovery of a useful drug or chemical and its preparation for profitable marketability, and there was no way the division could be prodded into erasing that inescapable fact. If one were in the chemical research and development business, this fact of life had to be built into business calculations. To pretend that one didn't know about the lag between discovery and applicability marked one as foolish, naive, or perverse. The profit exigencies of the conglomerate had obviously become more important than the orderly and traditionally sound operation of the research division. If the salesmen and the controllers were running Spectrum, they were also running Gimex. It wasn't the Gimex team that ought to have been indoctrinated in the ways of Spectrum; it was the conglomerate wheeler-dealers who ought to learn just how a research division operated. The president knew all too well that Spectrum was waiting for Government approval to market a Gimex-conceived product for which its managers had high hopes, but that approval was not coming soon enough to assuage the greedy stockholders.

The Gimex president's response was superficially understanding, but essentially unsatisfactory. The division was to produce profit, and fast. The rest of the company was doing its job; Gimex should do as well.

My young vice-president was enraged and he envisioned the stagnation and/or decay of Gimex. He got on the phone and requested a half hour of the Big Boss's time. My man, who was highly respected in the business, got his half hour, which the Big Boss happily granted as part of his continuing attempt to appear human while juggling the eleven precarious companies in the Spectrum conglomerate cache.

My vice-president made his case with the same ardent candor as he had at the Gimex meeting, adding that since president X had come to Gimex the smooth cooperation between scientists and marketing people had begun to deteriorate. There would be no restoration of Gimex's smooth functioning both as a scientific and profit-generating arm of the corporation until someone was at the top who understood the real Gimex story.

The Big Boss listened with apparent sympathy and asked for my man's recommendations for restoring harmony. My man gave them—chapter and verse in easily understandable specifics. The Big Boss took notes. Six months later, nothing had been done to correct the situation at Gimex and my man was passed over for his scheduled raise. Conscience and common sense caused him to submit his resignation.

I would never have learned the internal and largely secret forces of which my young executive's woes were merely the top of the iceberg if I had not been friends with the senior investment adviser of one of Wall Street's most powerful brokerage houses. The Big Boss of Spectrum was as aware of the shoddy treatment Gimex was being handed as was my young executive. But the Big Boss had other things on his mind apart from making Gimex continue as a top-notch research and development division. In order to finance the increasingly onerous capital costs of Spectrum's other industries without seriously diluting the value of Spectrum stock, the Big Boss decided to cut the operating costs of Gimex, which couldn't be counted on to come up with a readily available profit within the next two years. What my young executive couldn't know was that the Big Boss was secretly negotiating a takeover bid with another corporation. The better off the short-term profit picture was at Gimex, the more favorable would be the price received by Spectrum. The Big Boss was making a sacrificial lamb of Gimex and was hoping to find a corporation with an appetite for doctored meat. The president of Gimex, who had been so avidly attacked by my young vice-president, had been ordered by the Big Boss to take the repressive measures he had. He also had to bear the apparently justified criticism in silence.

My man's self-righteous and wholly good-willed criticism of Gimex policy was based on his assumption that he knew the big picture. He didn't. In order for him to understand the full story, he would have had to be given information which was none of his business. The lesson: If you want to criticize corporate-level officers, make sure you're a corporate-level officer. If your criticism is wrong because you don't have enough information, you appear arrogant and your indignation naïve. If you're right, you'll succeed only in alienating all the executives in the line of command whose competence you've impugned. Unless you can play on a truly established personal relationship with top management or ownership, no amount of competence or goodwill can balance the harm done by operating boldly beyond your jurisdiction.

One of the most maddening, if instructive, tales of executive capability becoming corporate misfeasance was chalked up in a company which had manufactured exclusively for the aerospace industry. The chief engineer of the company predicted that the multi-engine power plant that the firm was developing for aviation and marine applications would result in losses to the company going into tens of millions. After presenting his arguments within the producing division and finding no serious listeners, he started a campaign of memoing corporate-level vice-presidents. He was told that his predictions were based on insufficient information, and to go back to the job for which he was hired. However, he became such a source of irritation to his superiors that without ceremony and subterfuge he was fired.

His predictions were borne out with terrifying accuracy, and the losses that ensued stand as one of the largest single year's deficits in American corporate life.

A happy footnote to the story is that he was hired back eighteen months later—the moral being that it's all right to notice that the King is naked as long as you don't make an issue of it at the annual stockholders' meeting.

Some corporate executives cherish their prerogatives in direct proportion to the flimsiness of the grounds that justify their having them. And under these circumstances, doing a vital favor for your superior may be disastrous, as it was for a bright young man who worked in the office of general finance and operations of one of Manhattan's well-known magazine houses.

In this sizable company, the office of general finance and operations was where the heavyweight financial controls were administered and where top-level operating policy was determined. Accountants, auditors and various corporate staff would monitor day-to-day accounting and operating procedures, but the vital matters on which the corporation's existence depended were executed in general finance and operations.

Within the office of general finance and operations were three men who are central to this episode. The young comer I mentioned reported to the business manager. The business manager reported to the general manager of the magazine. The general manager was the man who was responsible for making the whole thing happen. Ultimately he was the one who must ensure that the magazine turned a profit.

Among the responsibilities of the business manager were counted the ten freight cars of paper, valued at half a million dollars, needed to print each edition of the magazine. On one occasion, a phone call came down from the general manager asking where in hell the ten freight cars of paper were. The Chicago printing plant was ready to roll, and if they didn't get the paper in thirty-six hours, there wasn't going to be an issue. This crisis couldn't have come at a worse time, because the business manager couldn't be found. Finally he was reached at his home. When told of the crisis he asked the young executive, his assistant, to handle the problem.

The young man did, digging through the business manager's files in order to find the freight slips covering the shipment in question. Finally he was able to get in touch with the right freight forwarder, and the ten cars of paper were discovered stalled at a siding in Minneapolis. Emergency measures were taken to get the stock rolling, and the paper arrived at the plant in plenty of time for the new edition.

The next day, the business manager who had delegated the difficult task of finding the paper to his assistant called him into his office and informed him that it was bad form to go through his files. Not long after, the assistant was assigned to another division. Rather than accept the new assignment, he quit—wisely, I think. He is doing well in another company.

When top management goofs off, it is likely that a subordinate's efficient solving of a problem will embarrass top management sufficiently to win him their anger rather than their gratitude. There's no adequate way for a competent, conscientious manager to protect himself from such dangers. If he sits back and watches the ceiling cave in, he can accuse himself of an indifference that damages his own self-esteem. If he steps into the breach, he is taking another kind of risk.

I recognize the cynicism of my advice, but misfeasance seems to be more worthy of being judged "foolish" than malfeasance. The man who performs badly or maliciously is either incompetent or evil. He deserves his downfall. The competent manager who tries to change the ruinous course of events by resorting to solutions beyond the code of corporate practice is squandering his virtues with no hope for reward, and in service of men whose means of survival characteristically discount impetuous honesty.

One of the most subtle and instructive descriptions of the corporate way of doing things is this one from Wilbert Moore:

> An administrative organization is not established or continued for vague purposes of friendly interaction, but rather for objectives which can be clearly stipulated and the degree of achievement constantly or periodically appraised. Such organizations are generally badly equipped to fulfill all of life's functions or their members' interests. But they are equipped to accomplish limited functions that require complex cooperation. If more than one objective is part of the mission, it is unlikely that all can simultaneously be "maximized" in all situations so that a priority ordering is needed as the basis for choice in cramped quarters. [5]

My young executive from Gimex, the pessimistic engineer from the aerospace company, the helpful man in the magazine's office of general finance and operations expected their corporations to respond in a way in which they are almost always not able to respond. Their remedies threatened the continued *limited efficiency* of the corporation, either by pointing out the unpleasant assumptions that elevated limited efficiency into the *summum bonum* or by endangering the status quo by which top management prospered.

Though a large part of the education of a recruiter involves

---

[5] Moore, *Conduct of the Corporation*. New York: Random House, 1962, p. 23.

learning about the way frail humanity behaves under stress, there is a more substantive area of knowledge in which all recruiters, if they are successful, become experts, and that is knowledge of the intimate workings of major American corporations. No other group of people is as likely to know as much about the nitty-gritty of American corporate life as is the perceptive executive recruiter. Corporate recruiters do their business because corporations have problems, and the best way to understand an intricate mechanism is to watch it malfunction. Just as knowledge of the human organism is a result of studies done to identify pathologies, the business expertise of the corporate recruiter comes from his constant acquaintance with the failures and disappointments of partially or wholly diseased organizations. If it weren't for our ailments, there would be no science of medicine, and where better to find out about the married state than in a divorce court?

As I have said, our clients are often too timid, dishonest or stupid to want an accurate assessment of their problems, but when they are honest and intelligent, their candid description of exactly what is wrong with their operation makes us privy to the most intimate details of American corporate life. And from this intimate association with the essential problems of the corporation, I can offer these renderings of some of America's major industries:

Automotive: Crude, oriented to an ultimate market and distribution system which is crude—car hawkers, new and used—garage mechanics with abysmal service—a corny status symbol.

Hotel and restaurant: With few exceptions, no professional management—hacks. Although the Western International and Marriott people know how to make money.

Entertainment: Worse than hotel and restaurant industry.

Forest products: Highly oriented to property holdings in Northwest and Southeast—low-paying—talented people find it easy to be noticed and appreciated—depreciation from their vast real-estate holdings helps their earnings picture and leads one to believe they are better managed than they are—"back to the land" characterizes their management style.

Electronics: Fast-paced, technical, and highly competitive (as in the semi-conductor business), these people have to be good—and are.

Machine tool and related capital equipment: Inarticulate and unfriendly—an industry of grunters, very dull.

Management consulting: Staff-oriented, lacking in decision makers—companies poorly organized with high turnover. We tell clients what they already know in words they can't understand.

Computer services: Many marginal but highly overpaid people in this industry—because computers are the new panacea and because practitioners speak their own language and don't believe in interpreters, we assume they're geniuses; some day soon we'll find them out.

Chemical: Technical types, obviously—introverted—more concerned with production processes than marketing. A client and friend in the chemical business says this is the prevailing attitude: "Look at our beautiful, new huge plant; we don't know how we'll sell its output, but we sure do make it cheap."

Banking: A surprisingly swinging group, especially among the commercial-loan officers in major cities; still frumpy here and there, but coming on strong.

Investment banking: The one service industry that is more opportunistic than ours.

Construction equipment: Also somewhat crude but exciting people—accustomed to big dollars in investment, inventory, product development and attendant risk in selling to a fragmented, cyclical industry—construction; also technical—a mechanical product requiring great engineering sophistication and solid research.

Publishing (particularly book publishing): Unbelievably sluggish, insular, outmoded, provincial (too tied to New York), overpopulated with polite, mediocre companies.

Advertising: Though deserving of some of its criticism and populated with its share of out-and-out phonies, it is, on the whole, unjustly maligned—many fascinating people—a more creative, open, imaginative group than you'll find in publishing—the stereotypes in plays, novels and movies are boring and ludicrous. They are good, positive cynics —remember their clients aren't always prizes.

Consumer durables (like TV, HiFi, electronic organs, white goods and various appliances): Good merchandisers or they couldn't survive—but crude in a manner similar to the automotive industry.

Retailing (including supermarkets): Expects its managers to work 70 hours a week for coolie wages—what caliber of people do you think that would attract?

Railroads: Though former astronaut Wally Shirra reminds us that we all need them, the Penn Central debacle reminds us: How unfortunate!

Airlines: Railroads in the sky.

Consumer packaged goods: All-around most talented, most articulate, most intelligent, most extroverted, and best-paid managements.

As the face of American business changes, corporate recruiters will have to be on the lookout for changes in corporate needs that may require wholly new services from them. And one of the changes already several steps closer than the horizon promises to be a great one for me and my colleagues, and, I suspect, may cause many of us to fall by the wayside. But for those of us who survive, I think the best days our profession has ever known lie ahead, and we will be forced to give up to an unprecedented degree the worst part of ourselves. For, in the future, I see a greater demand for substantive expertise and specific, denotative advice than has ever before been demanded of us. Up to now, we have been looked to for robotlike churning of bodies, not for ideas.

In John Kenneth Galbraith's *The New Industrial State,* the evolution of the American corporation from an entrepreneurial bureaucracy to a technocratic organism has been eloquently analyzed. Corporations, which have traditionally depended on top management for the initiation of new concepts and the directives to implement them, have become so complex, either through conglomeration or assimilation, and so technically sophisticated and specialized in many of their operations, that no one chief executive or management committee knows enough about day-to-day functions of their "technocracy" to direct effectively its operation.

Instead of exclusive pyramidal flow of power and expertise from top to base, an entire arterial system of experts, each with a special and, within the organization, unsurpassed knowledge of the problem he is assigned to solve, passes on information and recommendations, which top management is free to ignore only at peril of acting stupidly. Engineers, chemists, market analysts armed with the most sophisticated data, physicists, architects, systems experts, all with a greater claim to authority in their fields than the firm's president, whose power often stems mainly from his equity, increasingly determine the paths in which the corporations, and therefore the corporate state, will move.

This reliance on professional knowledge is inevitable in our increasingly complex and technologically oriented society, and as the corporation comes to rely more and more on the technocrat, the virtues for which the traditional executive has been admired will change.

In the traditional bureaucratic structure the successful executive has been admired for virtues such as *stability,* meaning a willingness to carry out orders without resorting to whimsy or arrogance, such as imagination or innovative criticism. *Stability* usually translates into a higher virtue by dint of long service, when it is then escalated to *loyalty*.

The niche into which a vice-president fits so snugly is neatly hemmed in by specific job definitions and a clear line of command responsibilities both up and down. Because the people with whom he will deal in the course of his executive life are as carefully defined as are the scope of his corporate tasks, he is praised also for *his ability to get along with people*. Military relationships offer a clarifying analogy. A superior officer's relationship to all PFC's is the same, and for it to be any other way would be a violation of military ethics. For a major-general to relate to PFC Norman Mailer as if Mailer were any different than PFC John Smith is not cricket, and, within the confines of military interests, is not acceptable. But the simple, overriding truth is that Norman Mailer is vastly more than the coefficient PFC. In military systems as well as traditional corporate ones, individuals serve the system, and the system is the *telos,* not the man.

Within the traditional corporate framework then, *getting along with people* is even more important than being honest with them or demanding of them anything more than what the bureaucratic definition of the corporation function implies. Thus, the executive vice-president of a major investment-banking firm may get along with his West Coast regional manager without ever discovering that the regional manager writes music or that the regional manager has something to offer about training innovations for the entire corporate retail staff. The regional manager wouldn't want to be pushy, stepping, perhaps, on the toes of people upon whose prerogatives he may seem to be impinging—in this case, those of his boss. The executive vice-president knows that his hierarchical control would be endangered. So both men, *loyal* to their corporation and blessed with *the ability to get along with people,* ensure the perfumed stagnation of the corporate intelligence while winning praise from their bosses and gastritis from frustration.

A way of life goes along with the traditional bureaucratic corporate ethic. Conversation tends to verify truisms rather than to seek fresh topics. Reminiscence about the "great guys" and the "great times" they have had together fills sales conferences, instead of fertile speculation. Dressing styles are conservative, emulating the respectability of older men and avoiding the risk of calling attention to the individual behind the job description. Automobiles cannot range beyond the dignity of one's job slot. If the boss drives a Cadillac, the vice-president will go only as far as a Buick Le Sabre. The waste of spirit, the accumulation of hypocrisy, the drain on intelligence is frightening to behold. And one can only marvel at the fog of complacency which stands between these executives and an insight into what they have become.

The most valuable commodity in the technocracy of the new industrial state is knowledge, and it is knowledge which increasingly lies in the hands of professionals whose main loyalty is not to a corporation but to their profession. There is no value added to a quadratic equation correctly figured and relevantly applied by the fact that a Harvard man rather than a Sewanee man was the mathematician, or that the Harvard man is an egocentric snob and the Sewanee man a Southern gentleman of the antebellum school. Ask a technocrat a question and, if he chooses to deal with the problem, the only value he gives in return is the accuracy of his answer, multiplied by the importance of the question. His personality, his loyalty, his ability to get along with people are not what the fast-coming corporation values so much as in the past. It values his answers, and he can give those regardless of whether he drives a Cadillac or a minibus, wears tie-dye shirts or Sulka's, works nine to five or midnight to eight.

The implications of the knowledge revolution will be crucial to the next generation of corporate executives. And as brainpower, specific fields of expertise, imagination and independence become more valuable in the corporate marketplace, the corporate headhunter will have to learn well where his new quarry can be bagged. If he doesn't, he will go the way of rolltop desks and green eyeshades.

It will become increasingly easy to distinguish the phony headhunter from the honest one. As knowledge becomes increasingly more important than haberdashery, the phony's camouflages just won't work any more. The honest headhunter has got to map out a carefully planned and muscularly executed program in order to remain educated.

First of all, he ought to read the trade journal of each industry in which he has a client. He ought, also, to read the in-house journal of every firm he represents. After an assignment is over, he might give up on the in-house journal, turning it over to a subordinate who should fill him in on any important developments.

I would suggest that he hire a research director or train his secretary to provide him with articles from a wide list of journals which he would not ordinarily read relating to areas of his professional interests.

He and colleagues within his firm should be responsible for making themselves familiar with the contents of a certain number of journals. Quarterly or so, the firm should meet *en masse* and discuss what they have found interesting and/or important. An incentive system for an idea that turns into a viable consulting service should be devised.

No matter what the pain, the headhunter should probably learn a foreign language. One of the most significant developments of the past ten years has been the emergence of the multinational corporation. The day is near when as much business transacted by American-based companies will be carried out by foreign affiliates.

Lastly, I would recommend that the executive who truly wants to keep his mind imaginative as well as practical choose an area of study seemingly beyond the possibility of its having any practical application to his job (something like Babylonian religions, medieval architecture, Indo-European philology, vertebrate anatomy). The harried mind needs a place to hide, and in those moments when good minds are seemingly indulging an impractical pleasure, the greatest of ideas often strike.

You may be wondering if I myself have done all these things. The answer is no, but I'm working on a program and attempting a novel.

The executive headhunter views American corporate life from a privileged position lying somewhere between a fiduciary and a card sharp. In his most austere role he is authorized to analyze the most serious problems of American business life and to find the men most capable of remedying them. This trust is bestowed on him by highly paid corporate executives who courageously recognize that problems have gone beyond them and who have the good sense to delegate authority to trustworthy management recruiters. In his most Machiavellian role he is a mediator between executives who don't understand their problems and job candidates who don't care what the job is as long as there is a quick buck to be made.

Without a strong streak of irony, the headhunter is a dullard unprepared to distinguish between those who deserve to be handled like the fools or the mediocrities they are and those who deserve his most expert judgment and most candid emotions.

III. THE CANDIDATE

It is November, 1971, I am sipping a convivial highball in the protective comfort of my club. My companion, in his early forties, is good-looking, intelligent, wealthy, and unemployed. He has not asked me to find him a job, nor will he. His bankroll is intelligently invested and he is under no financial pressure to find work. I know, however, that he is bored, and that he can find satisfaction only in exercising his very considerable talents as an investment advisor in the securities business.

I know something of his history. He has been educated in the genteel South. His father is a bank president. With family tradition dutifully ingrained, he received his MBA from Harvard intending to use it in the service of the family bank. As often happens when sons are long-trained to follow in the footsteps of their fathers, he soon discovered that his happiness lay in walking a different road. He came to New York and Wall Street, where for several years he worked for one of the better investment houses. He proved his mettle but felt he wanted to operate more on his own. He moved to their Chicago office and quickly became one of the most successful retail salesmen of stocks and bonds in the city. Not only did he make large sums of money for his clients, but putting his own money where his mouth was, he entered the last five years of the 1960s with approximately half a million dollars in profit.

With melancholy but accurate prevision he saw a period of sharp decline for the securities market and a dramatic rise in interest rates dating from President Nixon's election in 1968. In one of the hardest decisions of his life, he advised all of his customers to get out of the market and sit out the recession. Those customers who didn't take his advice he efficiently and courageously put in the hands of other registered representatives.

My friend's pessimism has proved justified but his accuracy gives him no pleasure. Now he wants to get back into the money game, but with three years of unemployment, his record looks funny. I jokingly suggest to him that the most impressive résumé he can present is his savings passbook.

Partly out of personal attachment, partly out of professional admiration for his business skills, I will try to match him up with the right outfit. I won't accept a fee, though he has offered to compensate me for my time.

I mention this story because it is an exception to an almost inviolate rule: Corporate headhunters never start an executive search at the behest of an individual. Always it is a corporate client who initiates our efforts. It is important that a man looking for a job understand the reasons for this, because headhunters usually consider private overtures one of the most annoying inconveniences of their daily work, one that involves personal and financial embarrassment.

Headhunting is essentially a personal service, the success of which depends almost entirely on the quality and quantity of work put in by the headhunter himself. It is important that he spend his time on searches that are most likely to produce the greatest rewards in return for his time invested. He is paid for listening to corporations, not to individuals. An individual is looking for one job; a corporation for many executives. An individual is looking for a job that may last him a lifetime; a corporation is constantly hiring. It is always easier to find candidates than it is corporations, and corporations pay our bills. Further, by definition, being a management-consulting firm means just that. We work on behalf of mangement. There are executive-placement firms that represent individuals. Generally it is considered unethical for a single firm to engage in both practices.

It is true, of course, that working on behalf of an individual as a favor to him may lead us to corporate clients accidentally, but the path is relatively long and winding.

Once a candidate understands the financial facts in the headhunter's life, he can then understand why to approach him as an individual looking for a job is also to put him in an awkward social situation; because he may have the highest regard for your talents, the most sincere regard for your person, and still not want to become involved with your employment problem. If he turns you down he feels like a heel; what he usually does is accept your résumé and file it in the "good luck, Charley" folder, which follows Z in the alphabet.

If the candidate understands this basic reality of headhunting, he may be able to develop techniques to fool the headhunter and to get the most out of this strange love-hate relationship.

Only the shrewdest of candidates can sufficiently confuse, charm, or camouflage his relationship to a headhunter so as to alienate him from his primary responsibility to his client and become the cynosure of his searching eye. Here are some tips.

The very first day you arrive on your new job, start thinking about your next career step. Start working up a game plan for that day sometime in the future when you, just as countless thousands before you, will be fired, or will become so discontented with your corporate duties that you decide to leave. The earlier you begin the better, because the first year of employment is a honeymoon period where the chances of your being liked and supported are greater than at any other time within the next ten years. Do not count on your virtue to guarantee you longevity. Even if corporations were totally forthright and loyal to their employees—which they are not—their needs change and so do economic conditions. With these changes you may become superfluous. You may be fired or somehow diverted from the mainstream.

Just in case you think that this advice is cynical and is demeaning to your notion of loyalty or even honesty, picture yourself in this position: A corporate headhunter telephones you after you've been on the job for only one year. You know that he is an associate of a high-powered and highly thought of search firm. He tells you he knows that you are highly paid. Perhaps, he even mentions a salary range in which he assumes you work and he overestimates by $10,000. He can't mention the name of the corporation for which he is recruiting, but he tells you in what field it operates. It's just something in which you could be interested. He adds that your name has discreetly been mentioned to top management and that they responded to it with great enthusiasm. You tell yourself that in all probability nothing will come of it.

The headhunter tells you he recognizes that men of your ability and proven record are most likely not in the job market. Even if nothing works out, though, perhaps you'll be able to suggest some other men in your field who might be interested. And there is always the possibility that you, as an executive at your present firm, will want to hire a headhunting firm to recruit people for your own company. At least getting together can set the stage for some future negotiations in which the headhunter might prove useful. The headhunter asks if the next time he is in town he might give you a call, and if you have time, have lunch together. Do you accept the invitation or don't you? Do you accept in a candid way or in a covert, self-interested way? I suggest that nineteen men in twenty will accept the invitation, and that fifteen in twenty will hide their desire to be considered for a new job by going along with the sugar-coated obfuscations the headhunter has offered you, such as his hope that you'll suggest other men for the job, or that your meeting with him may prepare you to retain him for your firm some time in the future.

If you can admit to yourself that you would gladly accept the headhunter's invitation, you're not as content as you think you are, and you've got your own interest healthfully ahead of your corporation's. As long as you're doing a good job for your present company, the emotional and financial balance of payments between you and it are even. Feel free to plan for your own future.

One of your first steps in throwing an employment anchor to windward is to get in contact with a headhunter without making him believe that you have yourself in mind.

As a key executive at your present firm you will probably know when a corporate problem reaches the attention of management. Let us assume that in the course of your career, you've either met a headhunter or heard of one you believe admirable. It would be canny of you to speak with the corporate executive detailed with solving the problem and tell him about the headhunter, stressing your own connection with him and your belief that he might be just the man to consult. If it is all right with your boss, volunteer to sound out the headhunter and to do some preliminary research into the man's competence to deliver the goods. By so doing you will do yourself two kinds of favors. One, you will have taken a concerned and active part in helping your firm solve a problem that otherwise might never have involved you. Two, you will have, or attempted to have, provided a headhunter to do legitimate work for a corporate client, and in so doing introduced yourself to him in the best possible way.

It's wise to keep up the acquaintance, and there are many good ways to do this, but the most important detail is to cultivate the headhunter's friendship *before* you need it. In this way you will be dealing from strength and in no way impugning your corporate altruism.

If you are in charge of a seminar for your firm, or can organize one with you as the volunteer chairman, you can invite your friend the headhunter to address the group on some suitable topic, not only with the hope of learning things from him, but to acquaint him more thoroughly with the staff of your corporation—men it might be important for him to know in his future consultantships with the firm.

If you are asked to prepare a paper or deliver a speech on a facet of your corporate responsibilities, ask the headhunter if he might put you in contact with some of the superstars he has met in his career who might be able to give you some special advice. Your conversation might go something like this:

"Al, this is Wylie Fox over at A to Z Products. The VP is still raving over that job you did for the food-products division. I'm glad I was able to get you guys together. Look, Al, I'd like to get some advice from you. The computer-applications seminar of the American Management Association has asked me to give a speech on new hardware and job training implications. It seems some joker over there thinks I really know my stuff. Well, I've got to admit I'm not totally ignorant, but what with every top expert in the field there and what with me the featured speaker, I'd sure as hell like to interview some computer-application people in the media selection field. I've got loads of friends who are just great, but I want to go to somebody new, somebody fresher, so I can get a new perspective. I wonder if in your travels you've come across somebody you really respect."

What you have succeeded in doing is informing me that you are highly considered in your industry; that you are modest enough to want to make a special effort, without resting on your laurels; and that you, in an area in which you are an expert, respect the kinds of men I have placed. Once again, you've brought yourself to my attention without referring to any employment difficulties. You might invite me to attend the speech, reminding me that some of the highest-placed executives in the field will be at the meeting and that you'd be glad to introduce me to men who might become my clients. If you don't succeed in getting me to attend the speech, at least you will send me a copy of the speech and thank me for the help I've been. Chalk up another gold star for yourself. Though I can never recruit you because you are with a corporate client, I will be disposed to help you any way I can if you yourself declare to management sometime in the future that you are going to seek a new job.

Or consider this: Let us assume you had introduced me to the VP of the food-products division and recommended that he retain (or at least made it appear that you did) me for his problem. Then suppose he selected another recruiter rather than me to tackle that assignment. The company you are with would then not be a client, and I would be free to recruit you if an appropriate assignment developed. You would have gained exposure to me while encouraging our friendship through your real or apparent efforts on my behalf. It may not be entirely petty on my part to observe that I might take a degree of semiconscious pleasure in recruiting you, particularly if you are a prize, from the company that spurned my services in favor of someone else's.

A top-level corporate executive with whom I've been acquainted for years has been baiting his trap for me and I've been aware of the addition of each tender morsel. And yet he has done it so skillfully that I'm still prepared to bite when and if he should ever need a job.

This man is the acquisitions expert at a conglomerate which has only recently sprung from a perennially successful trucking and transportation firm. He has a brother in Atlanta who is the president of an equally successful paper-products company. From time to time I have heard rumors that my trucking-company suitor has gotten all the satisfaction he can out of his $80,000-per-year salary and is looking for something to test his need for a challenge. Never has he confirmed this openly to me. When his brother's paper-products firm was holding an Aspen-fashioned business retreat, he asked me if I would like to meet the top men in the company and serve as a resource person. I was, of course, delighted. He arranged it with his brother, and never asked for thanks.

Less than a year afterward he called me and mentioned that his firm had actively been looking for acquisition candidates. Two companies which he had examined in depth seemed to have had all the earmarks certain acquiring companies would appreciate. The only trouble was that these two companies didn't blend in well with the mix of companies already in his own firm's conglomerate bag. He had a notion. he told me, that Conrad Components (a fictitious name for a company he knew was a client of ours) might be the perfect match for these potential acquisitions. Did I know anyone at Conrad who might want to hear what he had discovered? "Yes, I do," I replied and suggested he call the president and feel free to use my name. What my friend had to say interested the president of Conrad and the two men agreed to meet.

After their meeting, the president called me to offer his appreciation for introducing my friend and stated that indeed something might come of the business involving these two potential acquisitions. My trucking friend had hoped all along, of course, that he would have the chance to meet the president of Conrad under circumstances where he could demonstrate his skills in acquisitions, without looking like he was making a pitch for himself. He had sometime earlier concluded that Conrad was a company for which he could work contentedly. Naturally, he gave not the slightest hint to the president that this was his intention, but at this writing, it seems possible he may receive just the job offer he is seeking. If my friend were not talented and not able to make a significant contribution to Conrad, I would have expressed my opinions to my client and recommend that he not hire this man.

There's a proverbial disparity between the value of dollars and doughnuts, but I'll offer dollars if sometime within the next couple of years my helpful trucker (if not already with Conrad) doesn't ask me to help him relocate. If he does, I'll cooperate with my best efforts. It will be a matter of value given for value received.

Any executive who has the courage and the common sense to face up to the eventuality of his someday being in the job market will do well to lay the groundwork for his encounter with corporate headhunters, and the sooner he does so the better. But let us assume that you haven't been wise enough to cultivate the acquaintance of a headhunter. You're not stupid—it's just that like millions of other intelligent, well-intentioned people, you find it odious to live your life defensively. You have liked your job, you have trusted your bosses, you have given your best, and now, you have been fired, or would willingly listen to talk of other employment. You hear that guys you know, and some you don't, have landed jobs for thousands of dollars beyond what they were used to earning. They were generously courted by headhunters and treated with courtesy and deference. You wonder if a headhunter can really deliver the same bounties to you, if the executive recruiter really has it within his grasp to change the direction of your life.

These speculations are thoroughly understandable, compounded from legitimate wonderment that someone you have never met before can make a substantial difference in your material and emotional well-being. Can he do it? The answer is yes. Definitely. However, if you are obsessed with the wonderment of these marvelous changes which may accrue to you subsequent upon his granting you an audience, chances are you've got the wrong attitude needed to impress him. If you're simply modest, learn to get over it. If your modesty is merited, learn to market your strengths.

Corporate headhunters are not in the rehabilitation business. For that, see your local Yellow Pages under "Salvation Army." We hire good executives for better jobs at better salaries than they now earn. Any executive with half a brain will realize that the need for executive recruiters arises from a need for executives. We come to you because we need you. It's up to you to convince us that you're the right man for the job. The biggest mistake you can make, however, is to give the impression that you will listen to any job offer. The absolute primary requirement of a candidate must be to make the headhunter understand that he is not looking for any job. What he is interested in is hearing what it is in the job under present discussion that makes the headhunter think that the candidate would be interested.

If you, the candidate, *are* desperate for a job, hide it. If you, the candidate, *are* fearful that your present job is coming to an end, *hide it*. If you would go to work for less money, *hide it*. You are not being asked to tell all. You are being asked to make an honest presentation of what you have to offer, and if bad luck, malevolent fate and cunning conspiracies have combined to make your worth to your present company less than invaluable, chalk it up to happenstance, not to your intrinsic merit. Remember to make that all-important distinction between honesty and confession. I want to hire you for your strengths. I am not a priest. I am a businessman. Let's talk about what you can *do*.

The confident job candidate with a self-explanatory record of excellent achievements doesn't need to learn anything more from a recruiter than what the job is all about and what the compensation will be. He then decides whether or not he can afford to change jobs. He may decide, of course, that the client is a jackass, but he'll gracefully let the get-acquainted luncheon come to its end without embarrassing me as to the futility of my courtship. That guy's lucky, so why talk about him?

What you're worried about, if you are like the rest of frail humanity, when you meet a headhunter, is how to keep your faults from him. You're concerned that he'll know that you're scared, or that you're wondering how to send your kids to college, or that he'll think you drink too much. If you weren't concerned about these things, you wouldn't be human. If you don't learn to deal with them, however, you're not going to impress him.

There has been a certain psychoanalytic bias made popular in the last decade, which I think has overstepped the rules of social courtesy and introduced private standards into areas of business where they are irrelevant—indeed, harmful and in bad taste.

Because in business organizations rational behavior is expected the unconscious comes to be regarded as an indecorous and potentially subversive part of a man's mind. The ideal executive is the man who gets up at 7 A.M., and after a healthy breakfast, arrives at the office and puts in a full day trying to cope with his corporate duties. At night he is allowed relaxation, but it is understood that he will not do his job faithfully unless his business life is not far from his mind. In the dreams of the ideal executive, the day's work reappears as unchanged as an instant videotape replay. No bestial sexual desires, no repressed homosexual fantasies, no thinly disguised Oedipal plots, no castration fears, no scenes of violent retribution, no megalomaniacal ambitions. Neitzsche, speculating on the character of the Superman, pictured him as dreamless, because dreams are the fulfillment of unlived wishes, a sublimated sop to deeds of which we are incapable. For the Superman, it can be surmised that the daily routine of deed displaces wish.

Myths are no less important because they are based on illusions. It only takes an illusion that coerces people to make the illusion operable. Take the myth of the perfect corporate type. He is sincere, not because hs is *trying* to get you to buy a product or to induce you to support a venture of his, but because he really *believes* that what he is telling you is true, and not only is it true but it is good. He isn't *trying* to be sincere; he can't help it, because what he is selling you is good and it is good for you; he may be making a profit, but that is the way one promotes the Darwinian perfection of goods and services. What this predisposition in favor of sincerity and single-mindedness fails to take into account is that most businessmen don't feel like this at all, and that they may be coming up with the most splendid business results for the most dastardly of motives. Anyone with the slightest grain of common sense knows this, and to know it is to be fully aware that the difference between underlying attitude and performance may be dramatic.

Whom do you want on your Vietnam patrol, a sadistic, flag-blind redneck or a Harvard Business School graduate? But whom would you prefer in your living room? Whom do you want to defend you in front of the IRS? A professor of law who has written extensively on the differences between Far Eastern and Roman jurisprudence or a shrewd, roughshod, deal-making tax lawyer? Yet whom do you want to introduce to your family? The answers to these questions come easily.

Clearly most men do not define themselves by their actions alone. Yet in the corporate world, executive leaders not only want their employees to do right, they want them to think right. We are not supposed to admit to complexity, to this disparity between what we do and what leads us to do it. The deep reasons for an architect's interest in building tall, slim skyscrapers may be such, as Wilbert Moore says, that properly they should be left out of polite conversation, and yet not affect his disciplined use of the rigorous logic of his trade. Why then should a corporation intending to hire him send him to a psychologist who will test his responses to stimuli intended to uncover penis envy? Why should a man subject to periodic depressions, yet never sloughing off at work be forced to admit them? Why is a man who tests out as a hater of dominating women forced to safeguard his reputation by lying about homosexual reveries?

A corporation has a right to know what you are capable of achieving on the job. Their speculative forays into psychologizing are obnoxious.

For over three years, I was a counselor working with emotionally troubled adolescents under the supervision of a psychiatrist. At the same time, I was taking advanced training in counseling and personality theory at the Alfred Adler Institute of Chicago. This background has been helpful to me. However, uncovering personality traits through extended psychotherapy and the discovery of how these traits hang together as a psychic system and how they might impinge on areas of life such as job, marriage, friendship etc., is far different from a battery of tests and a two-hour interview by a psychologist employed by a corporation. I am in favor of therapy, but not in favor of industrial psychologists who pretend to omniscience.

Professional industrial-psychologist firms are like the rest of us in consulting. They are poorly managed, have high turnover, and don't do any better than the rest of us in selecting personnel for themselves or their clients. They are no worse; the point is, they aren't better.

The job candidate should never feel himself obligated to "let it all hang out." He should confine his conversation to job-related specifics, and it is his duty to himself to play-act if he feels his personal life is being voyeuristically peeped at. If you want the job for which you are interviewing, tell the headhunter or psychologist what he wants to hear whenever he shifts from permissible questions of commerce to questionable ones of personality.

The countenance of the corporate man shines forth his homogeneity and advertises the reassuring notion that behind the business façade there is a deep substratum of more façade. Why this frightening concoction should have become virtue has deep historical and cultural ramifications. It is difficult for us Americans to remember that it is not universal that a man be defined by his work. The most useful definition of the concept "gentleman," was in England—at least until recently—a man who didn't have to work for a living. The Greek city-states, to which we Americans commonly refer for our notions of democracy and excellence, justified slavery on the grounds that it freed the citizens from the grubby necessity to work with their hands. Stendhal, constantly in debt, writing books destined to earn him less than a pittance in his lifetime, came back from England in bewilderment: My God, he thought, the English spend their days working for a living! He could think of no greater odium. The rabbi in the Eastern European *shtetl* paraded as a privilege of his elevation his freedom from all physical labor, and his ignorance of how things worked in the world as a characteristic of his spirituality.

It may be ultimately wrongheaded to define man in terms of his labor, making him *homo fabritor* (man the worker) rather than *homo sapiens* (man the thinker), but it is, I suppose, a necessary attitude in a capitalist society such as ours. What is odious, however, is to create an image of the corporate executive in which his virtue is inextricably bound up with his occupation and then demand from him in psychological testing and in job interviews the kind of candid revelations about his subconscious, the recognition of which obligates the interrogator to acknowledge a much more complicated (humane) definition of personality than that with which the corporation is willing to deal. All of which goes toward justifying my apparently shocking advice, which is that no psychologist has the *right* to find out anything "important" about you, and neither does any corporation. They may find it useful in their dealings with you, but the granting of this knowledge to them is a privilege you bestow, not one they have a right to demand.

It is quite unlikely that the qualities which would make the headhunter like you as a human being are the ones which will most importantly figure in his and his client's decision to hire you. Yet, since the most natural and one of the strongest emotions a prospective job candidate feels is a desire to be liked, he may find himself trapped into soul-searching revelations and deep, candid evaluations of his personal worth. Resist the temptation.

Since the conversation between you and the headhunter should be limited to the specific business matters before you, with a leavening of amiable small talk thrown in to make it seem that you are both enjoying yourselves, your conversation will probably fall into a time-honored rhetoric which both you and the headhunter have heard many times before. Don't be embarrassed by it. The game of candidate rhetoric is fine to play; after all, it's one we headhunters constantly play with our clients. Danger exists only when we think someone is really listening.

Many candidates tell us "they are not looking for a job," that "they are happy and challenged in their present job," and when we first call them that "of course they have not prepared a résumé." This kind of response, though sometimes true, is usually not. It is designed to convey an, at best, passive interest in the job. If, after exchanging the usual pleasantries, we learn aspects of the executive's track record that make him an attractive prospect, and we tell him that we would like to meet him, we usually hear a reply something like "Well, of course, a man has to be crazy not to listen."

In short, there is a striking uniformity in the oral responses to the first inquiry we address to prospective candidates, and in its familiarity we feel a certain comfort. The smart candidate will not be offended by the emptiness of this give-and-take; he will rather see in it something like the feather-preening and breast-swelling that goes on between peacocks before they get down to what's really on their minds.

One of the most beautiful and melancholy moments of indiscreet honesty I have run across in my career came from a man whom I have always admired.

This man was a minister who had left the pastorate of his own volition. When one of our clients, a creative type with an articulate management team, wanted a free-thinking imaginative person as a personnel director, I immediately thought of my ex-ministerial friend. He had left the ministry to become a personnel trainee of a major company in Chicago. He had done well, had even managed to become the senior personnel officer. But after five years he became disinterested in the company and took a job as a social worker at a juvenile detention home in Colorado.

He said he was interested in the job I described and would

fill out our biography form giving us a clear and detailed work history. It is our practice to take the biographical material, verify it, organize it, bind it in a nice folder and send it to our client. When I got the form back from him, it was enclosed with the following letter:

Al:

This résumé I've sent you is simply horrible. There is so much to say, yet what is said seems terribly incomplete. It gets harder to say what you have done and not done because it doesn't seem to mean much. At times I feel that many fine things have been achieved, yet doing them seems so much more important now than it did then. Will arriving ever complete the journey, or the final act ever be as important as the endeavor? Walt Kelly once said "All the fun seems to be in the running," not the breasting of the tape.

At forty, I sometimes feel old and begin to think that perspective is so much crap, that the less one sees the better off he is; that anticipation makes perspective reek like a rotting frog. You know, my friend, convenant theology is the only way to live. Travel light, but keep traveling; keep your thoughts on the uncertainty and excitement of the pilgrimage. *Homo Viator*. A man who travels. You simply cannot avoid experience, and with nearly any intelligence, critical judgment will come. You can't avoid it even if you want to, so that's no big whip. Good judgment is a crock. It just has to happen.

I guess that is one reason why I so hate a form like this. Life is reduced to a few words on a sheet of paper, and events that were wonderfully rich in your life now seem like an ancient ruin. You can sense the fun and excitement of making something happen, but what you actually did means little. Trivial. Like Sandburg's "Grass," it covers all.

At the training school, hearing cases, reading jackets, making gut decisions—sometimes based on pure hunch—that makes a day. Writing about it is as antiseptic as the kitchens of Sara Lee.

That part of the church really stinks because the only thing that ever really made it worthwhile was human suffering and the occasional sacrifice on your part or another's—the few times you really were needed—when you counted and when you didn't screw it up, when you really had courage to do it the right way in a clean, simple, honest way. All the other—the daily hustle, the baloney, the impression, the big show, all the stuff you can put on that lousy résumé—that stinks. You take ten years of the ministry and it stinks, for what really matters doesn't make a buck, doesn't organize, or train like some damned fascist. What matters doesn't get you anywhere. That's why it stinks too. You can't put down that sometimes you think that we are all crazy as hell, running ourselves to death, that we are deaf, dumb, and blind, and would expose our souls on a piece of paper for some lousy job, but get uptight at the thought of shouting obscenities in front of City Hall. In fact, we would get tossed in jail for that. Think we may get tossed in hell for the other?

I hope you can make enough sense of this résumé to make it interesting. But since you are so smart, you will be able to. Right?

It will be fun talking with your client. I have to get back on the stick and this exercise has prodded me. The last two years have been valuable, but the lesson is learned. The rest carries the promising smell of stale cabbage.

One phrase in his letter recurs to me: "... expose our souls on a piece of paper for some lousy job." The adjective "lousy" was an emotional rather than a rational description. The job wasn't lousy at all, and neither was my man being *asked* to expose himself. That demand came from within himself. If it *had* come from the corporation or from me or anyone other than himself, he would have had every right in the world to withhold his candor. There is, however, one situation in which a candidate may find this kind of soul searching demanded of him, and I want to give him advance warning so that he can handle the situation with the firmness and disdain it deserves.

Many corporations demand that executive candidates take an extensive series of intelligence and attitude tests. These tests often run six hours and more. To the extent that they test I.Q., language facility, knowledge of specific disciplines such as mathematics, spatial relations, finance, etc., they may be helpful; certainly they are at the very worst only boring. Scheduled with the battery of tests, however, and usually administered at their very end, when the candidate is probably tired and unwary, is a personal interview with the psychologist. In the hour or two you spend with this stranger, he asks you questions and observes the content and the manner of your responses so that he can deliver himself of his opinion about whether you are or are not suitable for the job. Armed with the quickly tabulated results of your tests, he feels he has a real opportunity to see of what you're really made. He will be thoroughly unembarrassed by using his title of psychologist to make you believe that his interview, as all *medical* ones, is privileged and that total honesty is absolutely necessary because to lie to your doctor can only work against you. He will make you believe that it is your interest he has in mind. *Don't believe him for a second.* He is reporting to a firm who pays his fee, and what he is trying to determine is whether or not you'd be good for the job.

Picture yourself having spent many hours with the corporate headhunter talking about your qualifications and the demands of the job for which you're interviewing. You have a long record of superior service behind you. You have met with the corporate client, probably traveling some distance to do so, and in all likelihood causing you to make up some falsehood at your own company about why you would be away from work. There seemed to be good rapport between you and the client. Now you are sitting in front of a man who knows little or nothing about your business skills, but who, armed with the cachet of his professional achievements, is going to make a decision about you which may have crucial bearing on your employment.

The psychologist's interview is an attempt by the corporation to reduce risks, but the interview usually turns the best people off. If a star candidate declines interest in a job because he resents the whole psychological approach, a client may be depriving himself of an outstanding answer to a corporate problem because he insists on a psychologist's report. If the skeptical candidate does acquiesce, and undergoes the examination, he is usually hostile about it, and shows it. The psychologist senses it, usually becomes defensive, and writes a negative report because of his understandable bias.

One candidate did deep-knee bends, juggled his pencil, and paced the floor during a consulting psychologist's interview. He later told me that the idea of seeing a psychologist was ludicrous. But he wanted to have some fun with the client, psychologist, and me, since we were obviously willing to have fun with him. That fellow, by the way, rejected by psychologist and client alike, has gone up to a highly successful general-management post with a well-known, profitable firm. I get much more enjoyment out of such a tale than I did out of a psychologist's interview with one candidate who has since become my close personal friend.

The job under consideration could have grossed my man about $50,000 the first year, and within five gone up to more than $75,000. My candidate was twenty-nine years old! He was understandably anxious to make a good impression. He had been interviewed in Chicago for two days by every executive who in any way might have a connection with him. Day and night he was in the spotlight. Just when he thought that the last inquisition had taken place, he was sent off for four hours of extensive intelligence and attitude tests. The last hour was the interview with the consulting psychologist.

My friend is a particularly candid fellow, and this natural tendency, coupled with his having gone through several years of psychoanalysis, set him up perfectly for the psychologist, who in this instance was to use his professional credentials for no more elevated purpose than acting as a corporate peep.

My friend was asked to make himself comfortable while the psychologist looked attentively at the personnel forms my friend had dutifully filled out: education, place of birth, previous jobs, level of compensation, hobbies, etc. The first comment the psychologist made was, "Well, Mr. Henry, I see that you go by the name 'Bill' when none of your three names is William."

My man thought that comment was rather odd. "Remarkable observation," he thought, especially since he had clearly written this nickname on the questionnaire. "And what school did you attend, Mr. Henry?" Odder still. That too was clearly written. My friend, wanting to appear cooperative, dutifully reaffirmed what needed no reaffirming. The psychologist asked several more of these superfluous questions, all the while sitting with the answers to them clearly recorded on the questionnaire he held in his hands.

The next question was, "Tell me something about your mother. Did you get along? Do you respect her? Just talk off the top of your head."

My friend became flustered and the easy, matter-of-fact

response he had made to the previous questions, plus the "professional certification" of the questioner, made it difficult not to answer this last, personal question just as candidly as he had the previous minutiae. Not to answer would imply that he was willing to be candid only about unimportant matters. With great embarrassment and a sense that he was being had, Henry told about the chaotic feelings he had about his mother, and the mixed admiration and hate he felt for her. The psychologist listened with amiable professional detachment.

"Now, Mr. Henry, what kind of estimate would you make of your net worth?" The psychologist had switched gears again, and because he had now established his right to know about deeply personal matters, how could one deny him financial information? Henry, who should have told him off, dutifully answered.

"Let's get around to your father. What are your feelings about him?" This question was followed by "Does your present firm pay for your club memberships?" That question followed by "Are your sexual relationships satisfactory?" And that question by "What is the most money you have earned in one calendar year?"

In the excitement of the two-day interview, in the tenseness of thinking that the job was going to be his, Henry let himself be abused by a psychologist who was using his privilege to bully private information out of him.

Henry returned to his home in New York, and gradually it dawned on him how he had been humiliated. In anger, he called the manager (who announced *he had decided to hire him*) and vented his disgust on him. Gratifyingly, with a sense of integrity, Henry declined the excellent offer. Some things money can't buy.

My advice to candidates regarding psychological testing is this: Do not tell anything to the psychologist that you wouldn't tell the client. If you must submit to personality testing to get the job, decide in advance if you can bear it. If not, in no uncertain terms make that clear to the corporation. It's pretty difficult to put a price on the dignity you lose when you submit to these tests against your will.

There are signs that business is waking up to the futility of motivation theory. Thomas H. Fitzgerald, Director of Employee Research and Training Activities at Chevrolet Motor Division of General Motors Corporation, calls his article for the July-August 1971 *Harvard Business Review* "Why Motivation Theory Doesn't Work." The subtitle is "We should discard the dismal vocabulary of motives, motivators, and motivation and think about becoming a society of persons." He concludes his article with this observation: "We look back now at personality testing, slightly incredulous at its colonialist mentality and its banality of concepts, wondering how we could have been taken in by its promises of penetration and mastery."

If my comments about psychologists appear overly critical and seem to come from someone who has been damaged personally by dealing with them, let me assure you this is not the case. Having a master's degree in sociology with a major in social psychology, having combined the counseling practice referred to earlier with a full-time college teaching position where I taught courses on deviant behavior, I was judged acceptable to assume the responsibilities of industrial psychologist with a celebrated management consulting firm. This was my first job in industry. I reported to a man who was head of the firm's personnel consulting department and who himself held a Ph.D. in clinical psychology. Interviewing for both this job and the one I was to move to after leaving this firm involved rigorous testing and interviewing at the hands of a psychologist. Whatever the criteria of measurement, apparently I "passed" and needn't be accused of sour grapes on that account.

In the thirteen months I served as an industrial psychologist on my first job, I studied and was trained in the theory and practice of psychological testing. I personally administered hundreds of tests and conducted a similar number of interviews. I remember a couple of projects I was in charge of that make me smile as I think of them.

On one project, I was commissioned to test and evaluate each member of the entire management team of a cement division of Martin Marietta Corp. I was asked to do this by the president of the division. I tested, interviewed and wrote a three-page confidential report on each of over forty people. The strange result of these tests was that on the mental abilities section all the individuals scored lower than the 50th percentile for their industry norm group. The test was given under normal circumstances. This assignment taught me that tests often simply aren't valid—that is, they don't measure what they purport to measure. I couldn't bring myself to believe Martin Marietta had a singular, monopolistic ability to hire dunces.

On another project, the halo effect often ascribed to psychologists for their observations was amply demonstrated. On this project, I tested over eighty hourly workers at an automotive-products plant of a Cleveland-headquartered corporation. The purpose here was to identify through testing and interviews which of these workers would make good candidates for foremen. My procedure was to interview the ten men who achieved the best composite test scores and make my recommendations for promotion to supervisory responsibilities.

The best personality tests have what is called an "objectivity" rating. This is a score that indicates how honest a person is in answering the questions on the test. The rating is determined by the responses a person makes to such "objectifying" questions as "Have you ever stolen anything?" or "Have you ever purposely hurt someone's feelings?" If a person answers a sufficient number of such questions "No," he can be said to be "faking" the test or lying on the test. His test has a low objectivity.

One of the ten men I interviewed had a low objectivity rating on his test and seemed unusually nervous during the interview. Over lunch with my client, I mentioned that this fellow faked his test and seemed concerned about something.

A few days later, back at my office in Chicago, I got a call from my client, who told me that the man we had discussed over lunch had been arrested the night before for making obscene phone calls to women in the community. The client went on to say that when he visited the man in jail that morning, the man told him, "I just know the psychologist was on to me and knew what I was doing." That client to this day refuses to believe I am not possessed of prophetic powers. What objectivity tests prove, however, is not whether a man is executive material, but whether or not he's honest. If top management had to go through the same tests as plant workers, many corporations would have empty board rooms.

Episodes like the above were duplicated several times over. That, combined with the staggering evidence that companies which selected executives without the aid of psychologists were as successful in predicting job success as those who used us or some other psychologists, convinced me I was in the wrong field. I made plans to leave the firm and soon thereafter joined Spencer Stuart & Associates, an organization which at that time concentrated on executive-search consulting. I note with irony, however, that before being made a job offer by Spencer Stuart, a firm which to a man publicly decries the use of psychologists, I had to undergo a psychological evaluation with Rohrer, Hibbler & Replogle—probably the most prestigious industrial-psychologist firm in existence.

As you might expect, some of my clients rely on consulting

psychologists in evaluating candidates we present. I must admit that on more than one occasion I have enjoyed the quandary I have placed a client in by persuading him to send a candidate to *two* industrial-psychologist firms for evaluation. What does a client *do* when he hears a candidate praised by one psychologist and vilified by another?

Earlier I gave you advice on how to deal with a headhunter and how to make sure you get what you want from him. Now let me give you tips which may be helpful in girding yourself for your encounter with the consulting psychologist.

The most essential requisite for proper dealing is to approach this encounter with the right attitude. Immerse yourself in the thought that you are an accomplished con man who is out to relieve a wealthy widow of her most precious jewels over afternoon tea in her sun parlor.

Additional clues for treading the psychologist's maze follow:

—Never deprecate your previous experience. No matter how poor, stress how much you learned and how it has made you a better man—even if you learned what not to do.

—Don't be flippant—take pains to go into necessary detail.

—Be positive, friendly, smile a lot, keep it light, assume the best, as if the exercise is actually enjoyable: "You always look forward to things like this because it gives you a chance to learn about yourself, providing there is feedback on the results."

—Be friendly, but don't talk too much. This creates a bad first impression.

—Don't volunteer too much. Make the psychologist ask the right questions—none of that nondirective nonsense—but don't get into a power struggle. If that happens, only you can lose.

—Let him know you think his client, your prospective employer, is loaded with integrity, insight, brilliance, etc.; that although demanding, he will be enjoyable to work with.

—If you have been presented to the client by a headhunter, cleverly, with a smile, say something slightly disparaging about him. If I had presented you, you might say, "Al's a good guy. I've known him a couple of years. He's a little grasping and gets the cart before the horse, but he seems to do a pretty good job." There is a natural hostility, I admit, between psychologists and headhunters, and it will help your cause if you let him know which side you're on.

—If he asks you what your net worth is, fib a little, if you have to—the fee he collects for an executive evaluation won't underwrite a Pinkerton investigation. Tell him you saw the recession coming and took your hundred grand out of the market.

—Don't mention eating and drinking a lot. If he asks, on the sly, about your drinking, tell him you have a drink or two at business luncheons when the occasion calls for it and that you have a cocktail at home in the evening. Most psychologists are looking for extreme oral needs. If you are a nail biter, keep your hands in your pockets.

—Watch out for those "objectifier" questions I mentioned earlier when you take the tests.

—At the end of the interview, finish off by telling him how much you have enjoyed meeting him and going through the exercise; that if you end up with the client, you look forward to working with him; that he should be a big help to you as a "new boy in school."

The hypocritical psychological interview is one of the most annoying abuses a candidate need be wary of. Here are some others:

1. Reference checking of candidate before mutual interest has been established between him and client, thereby creating the chance that word of his job hunt will get back to his present company and jeopardize his career.

2. We headhunters will sometimes encourage a candidate to meet a client even though we are almost certain the client will reject him. We are using him to contrast the candidate with one we really want the client to hire. Happily, however, we have sometimes been fooled, and the client elects to attract the candidate we were using as a decoy.

3. Sometimes, in order to get information about a candidate, we court other executives in the company and make them believe we are interested in them as candidates, when in fact we are not. Call it righteous indignation, but I honestly refuse to *use* people to this extent.

4. Many of us have been guilty of taking the short view and persuading candidates to take jobs with companies where the odds were that they would fail. But again, some of these people have fooled us and become enormous successes.

5. Matching up a rotten client with a rotten candidate. We have all been guilty of taking an assignment with clients whom we really knew we couldn't help because the job was too unattractive to quality people. However, one of our major clients today is a company with which I started work on that basis. The client learned so much from the first search, which ended in dismal failure when he was unable to attract anyone, that he brought us back for counsel on other matters in which his goals were reasonable.

There is no better way to impress a headhunter than to ask him questions which demonstrate that your prime concern is finding out what kind of a company he is representing; and the most sophisticated way of getting a good idea about what it will be like to work at a given firm is to find out something about its organization.

Unless you are a candidate for the top position in a corporation, you will be reporting to a superior. It is essential that the man to whom you report have an understanding of your tasks and that he be sympathetic to them. In many corporations, however, the top executive in a division may be a man who is simply an appointed watchdog of management or a man whose training and loyalties make it unlikely that he will know or care about your responsibilities.

A common instance of this is when the head of a technical operation, such as a metallurgy or chemical division, is responsible to an executive officer who is essentially a financial expert. He tends to reduce technical problems to financial ones. It may be difficult or impossible to make him see why the long-range development of an expensive but potentially lucrative process should get his support, when there are more immediately revenue-producing alternatives.

In another instance, your company may be organized so that your boss, who is sympathetic and knowledgeable about your problems, must report to corporate officers with whom his division has little clout; as, for example, a publishing division of an electronic media conglomerate might.

By understanding how the decisions are made in the division for which you might work and how that division relates to the total corporation, you mark yourself as a savvy executive, and one who really cares about what his prerogatives will be.

In a corporation where all recommendations must be passed from manager to manager until they reach the top, it is generally true that the competence to make operational decisions is inversely proportional to the eminence from which it is delivered. This is especially true of centralized companies in which the president, for example, whose successful route up the corporate ladder was, let us say, through marketing, now has the ultimate decisions to make on overall operations. He is almost certain to know less about the manufacturing problems of his turbine division than the plant manager of the turbine division, or his own vice-president of manufacturing on corporate staff.

How much trust will be vested in you? Of course, your own qualifications go a long way in determining that. But will your decisions about quality control be overruled by a tax expert interested more in depreciating older property than in upgrading present equipment? When you ask your superiors for a feasibility study of a new product which you would like to put into production, will you be told that your proposal is impractical, without being told that the reason is that the leisurewear division has been earmarked for a huge warehousing development? Will your superiors keep this information from you because the affairs of the leisurewear division are not your concern?

In short, the manner in which your company is organized will determine not only what your power will be, what recourse to expertise you may have, but also how much you will be allowed to know about matters that are at the heart of your duties.

A decentralized company in which divisions are run by division managers trained in the operations of their divisions and accountable to higher authorities only at quarterly intervals is the kind of operation in which an honest, knowledgeable manager, who wants to wield effective decision-making power without the need for Byzantine power plays, is most likely to succeed.

Determining the organizational procedures of the corporation might very well be the first subject in which you and headhunter most seriously become professionally engaged.

Another crucial priority in dealing with the headhunter is to establish clearly in your own mind what you consider the ideal course for your career. Are you what the corporate behaviorists call "career-oriented" or are you "company-oriented"? The jargon is obnoxious, but the difference to which it points is quite important.

Richard Martin, in the September 28, 1971, *Wall Street Journal* distinguishes the types.

> Richard T. Berg began his career as a meat salesman 22 years ago, and by 1969 he had held increasingly important sales, marketing and plant operations posts, had willingly uprooted his family for five transfers and had finally become the No. 2 man at John Morrell & Co., the nation's third largest meatpacker. He was obviously in line for the presidency eventually, and sure enough today the title on the door says Richard T. Berg, President.
>
> But the door isn't at John Morrell & Co.
>
> Dick Berg, now 45 years old, is the President of Hygrade Food Products Corp., a company that lured him from Morrell with the promise of a doubled salary, the challenge of turning around a desperately sick company and the opportunity of becoming the boss right now. He was found by an executive recruitment firm, which received $25,000 from Hygrade as bounty.
>
> Why would a man leave a sure thing at a solid, smooth-running company for a post at a smaller, teetering outfit? He liked the money and the challenge, Mr. Berg says, and also it provided immediately "a chance to run my own company."

Richard Martin quotes Eugene E. Jennings, author of *Routes to the Executive Suite*.

> The career executive defers only to the requirements of managing a successful career. An attractive job is not something in and of itself. What counts is what the job will do for him, where it will take him, and how fast. His career extends beyond the boundaries of any single company, and he fears having it prescribed by any company or institution.

Richard Berg's aspirations are contrasted with the "company-oriented" executive like "James McFarland, who spent 35 years climbing up to the top of the ladder at General Mills, or a man like Richard Gerstenberg, who has spent 40 years at General Motors, and is likely to become the boss at the end of the year." [This has occurred.]

> The path that Messrs. McFarland and Gerstenberg have chosen is still the most-traveled route to the top. It has been estimated that 60% of chief executives still spend most of their careers at the companies they end up running. But today's younger executives—men like Mr. Berg who were just babies or boys during the Depression and who thus feel they don't need to trade their underlying loyalty in return for the security of seniority—are more prone to hop from job to job in their search for success.

If a candidate knows whether or not the company is vertically structured (centralized) or horizontally structured (decentralized), and if he knows whether he is company-oriented or career-oriented, he is in a good position to make some crucial preliminary determinations about my client company's capacity to fill his needs.

If you recognize in yourself an irrepressible need for the top spot, you will find the path to the top difficult to negotiate in any organization, but no less so in a decentralized corporation. Your expertise may make you general manager of the plastic-products division, but you will have had so little contact with the power centers in the forest-products division, the recreation-goods division, and the foreign-investment branch that you will need unusual resourcefulness for your influence to become company-wide. If your ambition can be satisfied by mastering your particular field of expertise and rising to the top in the division of which it is the essential operation, a decentralized company is just what you are looking for. For you, it will be preferable to a centralized organization in which your judgments will be subject to the approval or veto of hierarchical superiors who know less than you do about your job. And if things fall your way, you just may be one of the lucky ones who goes all the way to the top. Even if they don't, at least you will have more fun in your quest.

In the decentralized corporation, power is diffused, and decisions are not made from top on down in a strict sense. All but the most critical decisions are delegated. In the centralized organization, however, the battle is more likely to be *mano a mano*. The ambitious career-oriented executive will soon learn who are in front of him in the pecking order, and will begin to play the game of hierarchical hopscotch and sniper fire. He knows just who stands in the way of his progress to the top, and will devise appropriate strategies to bypass or eliminate the obstacles in his path. One has to have the stomach for such ruthless self-serving, and one would do well to balance the benefits of the top spot against the nastiness of achieving it.

A short while ago, a candidate of grand personal ambition and matching egocentricity and brilliance was talking with me about the first vice-presidency of a mutual investment fund. His professional capabilities were superb and there was no doubt in either of our minds that he could do the job. He and I knew, however, that ultimately the only position with the fund satisfactory to him would be the top spot. In the spirit of professional candor, I told him I knew his ambition would drive him to the top or out the back door. He admitted my analysis was correct. If we were to continue our discussion with any chance of fruition, we had to discuss the chances of a *coup d'état,* and, that, of course, would forcibly involve me in a candid estimation of the men who barred his way to his career's consummation.

The delicacy of the situation required dexterity. My fifty-three-year-old client was the very man who would be forced to step up to chairman by virtue of my candidate's superior performance. My client's most trusted colleagues were the very men the candidate would have to seduce in order to swing the delicate balance of power. Despite my full awareness of these potentially internecine confrontations, I decided to recommend the man for the job, and fully brief him on what to him were the dossiers of the enemy. My client was no defenseless pussycat, and I figured that in the world of corporate in-fighting "the King must die." Further, what the candidate didn't know was that my client was actually considering slowing down a bit and wouldn't find the addition of a man with the moxie to pull off such a coup a completely unwelcome idea. But not without a spirited contest first! I was introducing one fighter to another fighter, and though I was betting on youth, the line was pretty much 6-5 and pick 'em.

But to look back on the questions the candidate asked me is still a bit chilling. "Does President Jones have a history of illness? Have any litigous matters, especially those within the jurisdiction of the SEC, been settled out of court? Who in the industry is considered Jones's most adamant enemy? Who is the strongest among Jones's subordinates? Does *he* have any weaknesses?'' And on, and on, and on.

My candidate got the job. My last words to him were ''If you haven't made the top in three years, get out. By that time your thrusts will either have been successful or will have so announced your ambitions that either you will quit or be fired.''

Self-knowledge is the most effective tool the candidate brings to a job interview. As I have said, it protects him from compulsive and indecorous disclosures; it keeps him cool in the face of the pseudosincere pitch of most American corporations; it shows him in what kind of corporation he is most likely to find fulfillment. The other thing it allows him to do is indulge unembarrassedly in the essentially banal courtesies and customary usages of the job interview. Since it is just as likely that an executive will be chosen for the right reasons as for the wrong ones, he should also have the intestinal fortitude to be the master of trivial detail. As I have said before, he should not be flippant. But there are other ways he can disqualify himself; and among the candidates who will fail I have come to be able to distinguish easily recognizable types. Make sure you don't get taken for one.

1. The Inconsiderate. Always late for appointments. I flew cross country to meet one prospective candidate for a very top job. The candidate had a fantastic reputation and I was eager to persuade him to look at our situation. We were to meet at the airport Admiral's Club and then go somewhere where we could talk privately. He never showed up, despite the fact that our meeting had been reconfirmed. I never tried to reach him but wrote him off as a slob. Some people think they can get away with such behavior when they reach what they consider the grand heights of business. I have noticed that with the real pros, the top men of America's largest and finest companies, courtesy is an unfailing rule.

2. The Detailer. Takes three minutes to tell you why he couldn't take your phone call ten minutes ago.

3. The Braggart. He made his company what it is today. I always figure that if he did, why is he leaving it, except that maybe what he made it was intolerable.

4. The Guffawer. He laughs so loudly after the second drink that everyone in the bar scatters for silence.

5. The Desperate Man. He'll meet me at the Memphis airport at 4 A.M. after a 170-mile drive.

6. The Cheap-shot Artist. He's not genuingly interested in the job, and I can figure this out after a short time. What he's looking for is a specific offer so he can go back to his boss and try to lever a promotion or a raise.

7. The Reluctant Debutante. He turned down offers from three separate clients over the years I have known him. But he is always ready to meet another client and go through the interview process again.

8. The Spender. One candidate with no outside income, who was being considered for a corporate controller assignment and who was then making $17,000 a year, met me at the airport driving a $7,000 fully equipped Thunderbird. I had dinner with him and he insisted on picking up the check for steaks and a '59 Château Latour. Anyone who can't manage his personal finances better than that would never get introduced to my client.

9. The Swell-headed Negotiator. One candidate, overly impressed with his worth, insisted to my client that he have a ten-year contract for a $40,000-a-year job. You have to be talking larger salary than that for that kind of a contract, and if what you're trying to accomplish by asking for a long-term employment contract is the appearance of gravity and dedication, you must be realistic about employment guarantees, not merely quarrelsome and arbitrary.

It is a safe rule of thumb that any job over $50,000 should offer a contract. If the job pays less than $50,000, don't press too hard. Below that level you may not be worth the corporate risk. Younger men and middle managers who ape their more elevated management colleagues in negotiating big salaries, options, and benefits have been reading the wrong books. Unless your job has a direct impact on profit, forget it. If you are in middle management, chances are there is someone around who can do the job as well as you can. I have found that most candidates overestimate their potential worth to a company and don't know how replicable they are or how quickly they can be dropped from consideration.

Even if you qualify for an employment contract, there is no guarantee that its provisions will protect you or the company that gives it. The recent examples of Semon Knudsen at Ford (he had a $200,000-per-year salary plus bonuses and stock options), Richard Zanuck at Twentieth Century-Fox Film Corporation (he was fired by his father, Daryl), and William Howlett, former chairman and chief executive officer of Consolidated Foods Corporation, point to growing employer dissatisfaction with employment contracts for new executives.

In 1968, Handy Associates, the New York-based management consultants, conducted a survey regarding the corporate use of employment contracts. Of over one hundred leading industrial corporations polled, 27 percent used contracts to attract top executives. The following year the percentage had dropped to 15, and a poll compiled in February 1971 showed a further dip to 11 percent.

One of the reasons employment contracts are falling into disfavor is that it is almost impossible to draw up an airtight contract that will stand up in court. Courts have time and time again fallen back on the standard of "reasonableness" in deciding for or against the plaintiff, and God knows that the last thing contending lawyers representing a shrewd executive candidate and a careful corporate client are likely to produce is a "reasonable document."

The more comprehensive the terms of the employment contract become, the more minutiae covered, the more careful the guarantees and the immunities, the more unpleasant negotiations become, at a time when the new executive and his new corporation should be building goodwill and trust. Pearl Meyer, of Handy Associates, illustrates the negative psychology of hard-fought employment contracts this way:[1]

> A company controlled by the chairman of the board and president recently sought to recruit an executive vice president. The chairman wanted someone who could take over in the top job as quickly as possible in order to avoid jealousy of any sort. A top executive was interested in the position, and at their first meeting he and the chairman practically fell into each other's arms. The chairman of the board said, "I would work for that man."
>
> The executive, who had a good job with a large Midwestern company, asked if the chairman would give him a contract. The reply was yes, and the two parties quickly reached agreement on basic terms. The contract drafting was then placed in the hands of their lawyers. The executive's lawyer kept thinking up new contingencies and new provisions until the chairman finally said, "I don't think this man has any confidence he can do the job. All he is trying to do is get a contract that protects him in the case of failure."
>
> On that basis the arrangement fell through. Thus, the first rush of enthusiasm for a new job was eroded by the negotiations of lawyers, each trying to get the best deal for his client but neither working for the best deal for both parties concerned.

---

[1] Pearl Meyer, "When to use Employment Contracts," *Harvard Business Review,* November-December 1971, p. 70.

A job candidate, by pushing hard for a tight contract —which is, besides, difficult to enforce—may alienate people on whose goodwill his success is largely dependent.

Noncompetitive restraints, in which a corporation tries to keep an employee who has close and frequent contact with customers and access to private company information from taking his inside knowledge and contacts elsewhere, are often written into employee contracts. They are very hard to litigate but corporations have a right to demand them. If an employee is hired to invent new processes for a corporation, the line between which benefits accrue to him and which to the company ought to be clear. And, of course, when there is danger that an employee with knowledge of trade secrets might pass them on to his new employers, an employment contract which enjoins him from so doing is justified. Except for these three cases, however, the most reasonable, the most easily agreed to, and the most enforceable is the termination allowance.

"The purpose is to provide reasonable financial shelter to the executive if the new relationship is unsatisfactory to either party, regardless of who is responsible for the failure. In this respect the device is similar to the new 'no-fault insurance' for automobile owners."[2]

Most executives will be satisfied with a six-month to two-year termination agreement. "With a fair termination allowance, the corporation can be assured of the executive's goodwill and enthusiasm, which should be part of the emotional atmosphere surrounding the new arrangement. On the other side, it gives the new employee security against a rapid change in management or unexpected firing without subjecting either him or the company to the unpleasant perils of negotiating and litigating an employment contract."[3]

[2] Meyer, *Ibid.*, p. 73.
[3] Meyer, *Ibid.*, p. 73.

The adamant demand for an employment contract is a pretension many executive candidates foolishly believe is a necessary part of their executive ambiance, and, quite predictably, the major issue in contract negotiations is compensation.

More than ever I am convinced that men don't work only for money. Nonetheless clients are foolish to believe that they can make quality executives change jobs without an appreciable—usually 30 percent or more—increase in their compensation package.

Executives like to tell their friends of significant pay increases, which they see as an expression of confidence in their performance. Executives who are convinced they are in a desirable compensation bracket, let it be known discreetly what that bracket is. More than the substantial value of salary, however, money is a symbol or measure of how they think their company values their contribution.

Stock options, or the chance to own stock, are sought by executives more for the feeling that they are part of the team, that they belong and are appreciated, than for the actual market value of the stock. Many options over the past three years have proved a poor bet. In strictly monetary terms, executives would often be better off to have the equivalent in cash and invest in the open market under the guidance of a quality broker.

I am not implying that executives are not interested in building their estates. They are, but at the same time, they are interested in having their management contribution recognized. A healthy estate, while providing for the financial security of one's family, is also a testimonial to a lifelong pattern of having been appreciated and rewarded by the corporations for which one has worked.

Even if a candidate can get away with it, I believe he is making a mistake when he insists on a pay increase that puts the job beyond what the job is worth to the corporation.

In the first flush of the hiring romance a candidate may get his way, but should things later prove unsatisfactory to either or both parties, the candidate may have priced himself out of the market in which his services are likely to be bid. A huge jump in compensation, even if it is instigated by the company—which may be deluding itself by thinking it is filling a post more vital than it is in reality—can be the most seductive of traps. Unless the candidate is certain that the corporation has an accurate notion of what to expect of him, he may be in the almost impossible position of having money thrown at him which in a very short time will be a cause of resentment and corporate disappointment.

Many men who draw much larger than usual salaries, *i.e.,* $75,000 upward, often take pay cuts later in their careers so that they may accept challenges which their current higher-paid posts do not offer. This is not at all rare, and I consider these men lucky; they know that money is an emblem of success, but not the essence.

Another consideration that downgrades the importance of mere statistical compensation is the tendency of a raise in pay to create a rise in living costs. When an executive changes jobs and moves to another city, he usually can count on a first-year loss, and his resolution not to buy a bigger house and furnish it more lavishly than his previous one is most difficult to keep.

Perhaps because the allure of the big pay raise has become so suspect to me, I tend to become annoyed when prospective candidates start outlining what it will cost them in personal, monetary terms to change jobs and move to another city. When they start itemizing what they can get for their present house and what a new one will cost, they are talking about factors totally irrelevant to what the job is worth to the hiring corporation. If you judge the job up for consideration worth tackling, and if, by chance, it pays more than you are currently making, you have a good deal. Take it if the chance is yours, and you'll have the price of your wife's new draperies easily at hand. If it does not pay enough more than you currently earn, you have a difficult decision. Whatever the balance you strike between the financial greenery and mental health, don't expect any company to play Big Daddy with your personal expenses.

New York City, which is an exception to most rules, is an exception to the advice above. The candidate moving to New York should have a cost-of-living factor built into his compensation schedule. Unless the company wants its new executive to come to work dressed in threadbare tweeds and to take his lunches at Nedick's, they will have to hype up his salary merely to keep him treading water. New York may be the richest city in the world, but it also is the most expensive, and the amenities of life are so lacking that one may have to send out nightly to a gourmet delicatessen for a pint of fresh air.

The executive who too closely associates professional success with the size of his compensation in employment negotiations is in danger of pushing beyond what is tolerable to the client corporation. And an equal number of executives err by believing that their superior education and professional training are a guarantee of security and recognition.

The MBA candidate is an instructive example. A wealth of statistical evidence reveals widespread arrestment in the career progress of MBAs. I believe that most men who get to the top in management have developed skills that are not taught in formal management-education programs, and difficult for many highly educated men to learn on the job. I know several high-level executives who consider the two years of business school a two-year prolongation of adolescence.

The attrition figures among MBAs is frightening. After three years, one-third of them leave their first employer, and an MBA who leaves his job before he makes a contribution commensurate with the company's investment in him represents a significant sunk cost. Business executives, increasingly aware of the phenomenon, are less likely to be impressed by the pretension of the MBA than is the MBA himself.

In a Special Report to the *Harvard Business Review*,[4] De Pasquale and Lange report that nearly two-thirds of those who left their initial employer cited as the primary causes lack of advancement opportunities, poor expectations for substantial job responsibility, under-utilization of their MBA training, and inadequate salary growth. Couple this data with the further observation that after leaving their initial employment MBAs tend to move to smaller companies, and one concludes that there is less correlation between education and the ability to get along in a bureaucratic corporation than business theoreticians would like to believe.

J. Sterling Livingston in his "Myth of the Well-Educated Manager"[5] claims that "one reason many highly educated men fail to build successful careers in management is that they do not learn from their formal education what they need to know to perform their jobs effectively. In fact, the tasks that are the most important in getting results usually are left to be learned on the job, where few managers ever master them simply because no one teaches them how."

The hostility among middle managers to the formally educated, theoretically oriented egghead is proverbial and still very widespread, and therefore a diploma, coupled with instant salary and management status, may hinder an MBA more than it helps him. That the MBA is encumbered in this particular way is not justified. He may be as regular

---

[4] John A. De Pasquale and Richard A. Lange, "Job-Hopping and the MBA," November-December, 1971.
[5] J. Sterling Livingston, "Myth of the Well-Educated Manager," *Harvard Business Review*, January-February 1971, p. 82.

a guy as any manager in the company. There has been too much wide-of-the-mark criticism by business analysts who look to the inadequacies of the MBA's education rather than to the realities of human nature to explain his corporate rough-sledding.

The MBA got his comeuppance in the '69–'70 recession, and there is widespread reluctance on the part of my clients to risk hiring him. The MBA candidate would be wise, therefore, to show his awareness of the MBA problem, and to reassure the headhunter and the client that he does not regard his diploma as an automatic entree to the inner chambers of corporate influence.

The De Pasquale and Lange report has a fascinating and important finding in regard to the female MBA. The turnover among female MBAs is about the same as males despite the obvious added pressures of marriage and children that a woman faces. Coupled with recent census data predicting a shortage of top and middle managers by 1980, this finding reinforces the contention that women MBAs represent a largely untapped source of responsible, committed workers.

The last bit of advice I would give the job candidate is hardly theoretical, and that is, "Don't lie." We almost always find you out, and once we do, your bad reputation makes an astonishingly quick circuit of the executive-recruitment world.

One candidate claimed to have a doctorate in metallurgy from a European university. When we wrote the university, they replied that the records covering the year he had claimed to earn his degree had been destroyed by fire a few years ago. Clever?

One candidate, whom I had highly recommended to a client, impressed me as a man of the utmost integrity, and the position under consideration required all avoidance of any shadiness. I had heralded this man's honesty at great length. When we routinely wired his college, word came back stating that no person with the name of our prize candidate had a record of attendance at the school. Immediately I called the registrar to double check, and my fears were confirmed.

In chagrin, I wrote the client to tell him the bad news that I was withdrawing the candidate's name from consideration. The candidate was out of town, and I asked his secretary to have him call when he returned. Later that day I got a call from the registrar, who told me that our man's file, along with several others, had been taken to another department for photocopying and had not been returned during the time of my inquiry. He confirmed all the data our candidate had given me. I dashed out to the mail room and, thank goodness, was able to intercept the damning letter I had just written the client.

Luck, chance, error—all enter into the success or failure of a candidate's job search, and no amount of professionalism will eliminate all these vagaries. If, however, the candidate develops the self-knowledge and the confidence based on his knowledge of what the candidate-headhunter-client dance is all about, he stands a good chance of getting the job he wants and deserves.

IV. **THE CLIENT**

The unique and invaluable asset a headhunter brings to any client is that he doesn't work for the client's company. In almost every large corporation in America there comes a time when only appeal to outside help can solve the corporate problem. The headhunter may know significantly less about the corporation's operations and personnel than a score of in-house executives. He may not be as bright or experienced as a host of others. He may not even be as highly motivated, energetic, or single-minded in his pursuit of solutions as many in-house executives. Assuming all these things to be true, even then he is more likely to perform valuable remedial services than any one individual or group regularly employed by the client.

Most corporate problems that drive management to consider headhunters are complex ones, usually involving more than one division or department of the company and usually extending from top to bottom in the personnel hierarchy. Any solution to these problems, therefore, has to be analyzed and effectuated by someone whose mobility and power is not circumscribed by his job definition. A brilliant and high-powered sales executive might be able to solve his company's chronic late-delivery problems were he to have access to warehouse dispatching orders, which under the present setup are the private domain of another executive whose authority may be questioned only from within his own department. Extradepartmental inquiries are looked upon as attacks on the warehousing and dispatching man's authority, and not only by the executive under attack. What is even more insidious than saving one's own face at the expense of yielding to sane criticism is the support given by all the other executives to any executive whose prerogatives are being questioned by a company employee whose traditional jurisdiction falls outside the limits of the problem under scrutiny. "If it can happen to one of us it can happen to any of us" is the maxim that makes executives flock to their winged colleague.

Konrad Lorenz, [1] the philosopher-anthropologist, has shown that if there is any common denominator of animals in groups it is their self-imposed demand for a clearly understood picture of where they stand in the hierarchy of their fellows. Lorenz shows that in baboon society a gesture (adopted from the sexual ritual in which the female baboon presents her incredibly colorful hindquarters to the mounting male) has become a nonsexual sign of submission to a more socially elevated baboon.

In the Berlin Zoo Lorenz

. . . once watched two strong old male Hamadryas Baboons assaulting each other in real earnest for a minute. A moment later, one of them fled, hotly pursued by the other, who finally chased him into a corner. Unable to

---

[1] Konrad Lorenz, *On Aggression*. New York: Harcourt Brace & World, 1966, pp. 136–137.

escape, the loser took refuge in the submissive gesture, whereupon the winner turned away and walked off, stiff-legged, in an attitude of self-display. Upon this, the loser ran after him and presented his hindquarters so persistently that the stronger one eventually "acknowledged" his submissiveness by mounting him with a bored expression and performing a few perfunctory copulatory movements. Only then was the submissive one apparently satisfied that his rebellion had been forgiven.[2]

If the offender had not been allowed to demonstrate his abject guilt, he would have been ostracized from the hierarchy of the tribe, in all likelihood suffering serious damage to his psyche. Order, more important than ego or self-assertion, is the highest demand of the structured society. In the animal kingdom there is no behavior more archetypical than this demand for order.

And in the corporation a similar hierarchical demand operates. At the expense of efficiency and self-assertion, most employees—even executives—will sacrifice all other corporate concerns to keeping their own place. Thus, a man without a place, a man who belongs to another tribe, is more likely to bring effective reforming vision to a corporate problem than is an insider.

Tribal flocking is both the strength and the weakness of the corporation. To make individuals whose concerns outside of corporate life are widely disparate identify so strongly with the interest of the corporation that they become members of the same family puts great coercive power in the hands of management. It also makes it unlikely that programs for change will be innovated within the group.

All of which is not to say that the corporate ties that bind are bad. Like the English, most corporations, if they are

[2] Lorenz, *op. at,* p. 137.

at all successful, are fairly adept at muddling through. The system may appear slow-moving and cumbersome, but the fact of the matter is that to move faster may be impossible without changing the checks inherent in all complexly structured societies constituted of members who are sometimes bright, sometimes not, sometimes open, sometimes secretive, sometimes sane, sometimes not so sane. To accomplish this may require dismantling an organization of limited efficiency in favor of one more efficient, but probably more erratic as well.

Despite warring board members, vain presidents, vice-presidential backbiting, professional jealousies among technocrats, gossip and goofing off among secretaries and stenographers, the abuse of foremen, and strikes by the workers, somehow the job usually gets done, not too badly and with not too many people getting irrevocably hurt.

Perhaps the first cautionary reflection a corporate manager should have when he first decides to bring in a headhunter is whether or not his company can operate as well according to rational planning as it has by the hit-or-miss techniques it has traditionally used.

One of the reasons for the failure of MBAs is that they expect a corporation to run rationally, and when confronted by the relative inelegance of corporate arrangements, they in their purist arrogance are either offended or baffled by the truculence and perversity of human nature.

When a corporate manager is sizing up a headhunter, he constantly must be wary, must resist being dazzled by analyses of what is wrong and by prescriptions for remedies that may make sense as casebook studies but that require a wholesale revision of the operation as it presently functions—*especially with the personnel with whom it presently functions*. It is easy to arrest the growth of a disease by killing the patient; the ideal remedy is not so drastic.

It is not unusual for a headhunter to try to impress his prospective client with his knowledge of the very best people in the business. He has faith that he can solve your personnel problems and he recites chapter and verse the talents of the men he believes he can deliver. Yet you as a shrewd manager know that were you to hire the best talent available your organization might soon be disrupted. Especially in large paternalistic companies like General Motors, IBM, 3M, GE, Procter & Gamble, and Caterpillar Tractor, the day-to-day operations are usually carried out by a collection of people of average abilities pulling together. As everyone knows, these companies are consistently profitable, and such management is better than superstars pulling in different directions. One of the first giveaways of a headhunter's superficiality may be his instant roll call of brain-heavy, uncompromising superstars. It would be best to pat such a man on the back, congratulate him on the high quality of his acquaintances, and start looking elsewhere for help. What the client doesn't need is bringing chaos out of order.

But the most serious danger of which the client need be aware originates not with the headhunter but with himself. Because many clients are unable or unwilling to define their real problems, they force me to feign agreement with their rationalized assessment while I secretly am addressing myself to what I suspect their real motives are in pursuing a new executive.

A good example of the need for prudent duplicity occurred when the executive vice-president of a specialty chemicals company hired me to find a national sales manager who would bolster their flagging profits. When, upon investigation of the company, I concluded that it wasn't a new sales manager who was needed, but a research-and-development program that would produce a better product line, I was faced with a dilemma. The executive who hired me was either unseeing or too frightened to identify his true business problem, and was unlikely to endanger his protective camouflage by listening to a critique of his operating strategies.

My tactics, therefore, became tortuous. This particular executive bristled with resentment at having come to me for help in the first place, and at my every attempt to offer an analysis he petulantly derided my opinion. His discourtesy relieved me of the burden of total candor, and, with the thought of my fee to assuage my atrophied sense of capital *T* Truth, I became determined to find the "right" sales manager for the job.

My next step would involve me in a more potentially devious assignment than my first. For, while my corporate client had defined the terms of his own continued and accelerated failure, the candidates I would unearth for the job could not know (unless I were to tell them) that at best they would be the right men for the wrong job.

We corporate recruiters often refer to our business as a "complex, unusually purposeful art," not only because we are usually unembarrassed at inflated rhetoric, but because it is sometimes true. And in dealing with my chemicals executive (no doubt a self-synthesized man) his determination to get bad advice made my dealings *complex* indeed and the means of achieving my purposes subtle enough to be *artful*.

If I read my man correctly, he would be displeased at the competent performance of an executive who addressed himself to the corporation's real ills. I also had no doubt that he would spitefully try to sabotage the new man's efforts. To have recruited an executive who was by objective standards the best man for the job would have been an inhumanity which no fee could tempt me to commit. But apart from ethical considerations, to have proceeded with the executive search, disregarding the personality of my client, would have resulted in my recruit being fired and my firm being viewed in the light of his failure. By refusing to handle this executive search, therefore, ethics and finance might be in harmony, and my decision would be noble as well as shrewd. Before I made a decision to disengage myself, however, another consideration gave me second thoughts.

It is likely that a client who is an habitual self-deluder, even in the face of acute business problems, is the kind of man who would resent getting expert help, but who might welcome a weak sister, someone who, though well-intentioned, wouldn't have the verve or inner-directed need for excellence that would compel him to shake things up. This kind of man welcomes the mass of the boulder he hides beneath, as long as the job means a nameplate on the door and wall-to-wall carpeting. Therefore, for the client who didn't want to solve his problem, I set out to find an executive content to toil long hours in not solving it!

Picture the scene, therefore, as I sit staring at our chemicals executive, the sincerity of my rep tie, the firmness of my squared jaw, the responsibility implied by my blue suit, the competence by my poised notepad, assuring my client that I believe every word he is saying, while behind the façade I think that to satisfy this client I shall have to deceive him, and that to win the confidence of my candidate I shall have to praise him for weaknesses that will make him perfect for the job.

A client must level with me; otherwise he opens himself up for a whole host of dangers, the contempt of the headhunter not being the least.

Ordinarily, the surest sign I know that my client is not going to level with me and is going to let me struggle and second-guess for any information I get, is when he leads me to his vice-president of personnel.

Whether this person is called the head of personnel, of industrial relations, of organizational development or something else, he to varying degrees in varying companies is responsible for the human resources of the organization. He can be the bane of my existence and I of his, or he can be of great assistance to me and I to him. Usually, the banes have it.

Historically, the job has been staffed by executives who have tried and failed at other functions. But the situation is changing rapidly as corporations learn that imaginative, compassionate handling of their personnel is the main determinant of corporate health. Up to now, most corporations have paid only lip service to this concept. Bob Palenchar of Swift & Company, a $3 billion sales company, and Theo Frederick of Playboy Enterprises, a $130 million sales company, are examples of the strong new breed of heads of personnel who are taken seriously by their managements.

Those directors of personnel who resent me do so because they consider me to be an interloper on turf they believe entirely their own. And because most of my searches require my having a close working relationship with the chief executive, personnel directors are additionally upset by my intimacy with their bosses. In annoyance they sometimes intentionally or unintentionally handle my candidates clumsily, making my job difficult and embarrassing.

Today, the larger the company the more likely it is to place strong people in the top personnel slot. These incumbents have been successful in their own right and have had distinguished records elsewhere in the company. Chuck Hall, of giant Continental Bank in Chicago, is a good example of this modern type. Men like Hall are human-resources professionals and are not at all queasy about a search consultant's involvement in corporate matters. They realize they have particular competencies we don't, and know we have some they don't. Further, many of them have designs on line management, and with a headhunter's help the problems we solve together will aid in their plans' coming to fruition.

In a corporation large and resourceful enough to need and

be able to afford a human-relations professional, top management ought to make sure they hire one.

The vice-president of personnel, then, often stands in the way of my effectively solving those corporate problems which top management has hired me to solve. But the difficulty at that level is nothing compared to the difficulty of dealing with the top, when the top doesn't really know that what is wrong with the company originates with the top itself.

One of the most subtle perceptions a headhunter is called upon to make is recognizing that the virtue for which the executive client is most celebrated—the virtue on which he most prides himself—is the virtue that is causing most of the problems at his corporation.

In the cast of corporate characters whom, as clients, I should have turned down, are numerous cerebral and talented executives who were killing their corporations with compulsive injections of brilliant strategies and personal charm. It is much easier to send an executive who needs to learn more about finance to financial seminars than it is to stop an executive who knows all there is to know about finance from applying financial solutions to every problem that comes his way—regardless of whether finance has anything to do with the problem. Like the sweater of the buxom female account executive which became tighter as client billings decreased, the more attractive the diversion the more pernicious the tactic.

When a headhunter runs up against a client who has dazzled his own corporation as well as the headhunter with his particular egregious virtue, it is dangerous, if not impossible, to suggest that what the company needs is less of what the client most likes giving. As I look back on the assignments which required of me such unprofessional capitulation, I know I would have served myself and my client better had I refused the assignment in the first place. The dangers to the headhunter are obvious. If he is honest, he will almost invariably offend his client and do little or nothing to help the company. If he is dishonest and confines himself to cosmetic, unessential things to say about petty problems, he is making himself a hack.

On one such corporate safari, an advertising client (and nemesis) was celebrated for building solidarity among his work force. In whatever agency he had worked, backbiting, crude ambition and pettiness had been reduced to a minimum. There was no problem too small for him to hear, none so large that he would fear to listen.

When I first ʼbegan to ask questions about my warm-hearted client, I was told that if a secretary were having menstrual cramps and thought it proper that she be allowed to go home, she could book fifteen minutes of the executive's office time to embellish her complaint. That my executive was gray-templed and six feet three, with the smile of a Hollywood matinee idol, did much to ensure a steady supply of unhappy secretaries.

I was told also that when one of his young and promising account executives was going through a frightening divorce proceeding which was causing him real agony, our executive kept tough business problems from passing over the distressed young man's desk and arranged an excuse for him to take a business trip to the Caribbean. And, to top if off, when the young man was away, our executive took on the young man's responsibilities himself.

These Christian gestures made our executive one of the best-liked men in the business.

I had been called in because my client thought his organization needed restructuring. I have since come to believe, incidentally, that an outside consultant rarely is in a position to be knowledgeable enough about a company to offer expert advice on how a company should be structured. No amount of interviewing is likely to produce the insight necessary to combine existing abilities, personalities, interpersonal relationships, technology and market demands for the sake of organizational effectiveness. A good consultant, rather, gets a client to focus on his problem-solving needs and do his own organization planning and structuring to meet those needs. However, I was younger in those days and knew all the answers. Accordingly, I took on the assignment without hesitation.

The client suspected that he was holding too many corporate responsibilities. No matter how hard he worked, no matter what kind of hours he put in on the job, he couldn't keep abreast of the hectic demands of daily work.

The problem turned out not to be organizational in a strict sense anyway, but was the client's need to be loved. This resulted in his inability to say "no" to anybody. What was additionally frustrating in my search for the real source of my client's problems was that all his colleagues had been so charmed by him that they had been blinded to the inefficient use he made of his time. And not one of his colleagues could bring himself to realize that perhaps the real reason he didn't answer memos promptly, or read reports until they were too old, was that he wasn't capable of establishing realistic priorities.

With such a man as my client, I couldn't even judge his intelligence. Everything that was good with the corporation was credited to him; all that was bad, the product of things beyond his control.

Finally, I had a breakthrough. The only flaw in my client's homogeneous saintliness was an occasional loss of temper. I was told these were very rare, but they were seemingly arbitrary and quite violent. "Against whom were they directed?" I asked, and after being reassured that the recipients were all to blame, and that my client had exercised more patience than could be expected of a mortal, I was given some names. I looked up two of the offending members, now profitably and apparently happily employed elsewhere.

Both former employees of my client were abrasively quick-witted. They had no kind words to say about my client. He was a procrastinator; he covered up a slow wit with the assuring smile of a father figure; he gave lip service to new ideas, but was frightened of change. The list went on, but the common denominator was that my client used his charm and his concern with the personal well-being of his staff to bury professional tasks for which he was either deficient in talent or to which he found it too demanding to address himself.

I spent two months with my client's company. And while my suspicions about his psychological makeup were quickly kindled, it was only by careful observation over the course of many days and watching him in the performance of many tasks that I concluded that my Mr. Nice-Guy was the company's biggest enemy.

The corporation thought it owed its success to his ability to keep the work force solidly behind him. I found this solidarity the by-product of inefficiency.

Another by-product of this client's method of operating was that all his associates emulated him. Criticism of a colleague, justified anger, impatience with inefficiency, were looked on as bad form. The mark of the successful company executive became his mirror-image of the boss's benign disposition.

I wish I could report that I came out of this assignment satisfied that I had laid my cards on the table. But that didn't happen. I hinted a few times at what I thought the problem was, and the more I did this, the more superficially he pretended to understand what I was talking about. Before I could make my case in a forceful manner, he was telling me how happy he was with my skill, and that he found me one of the most amiable men he'd ever had the good fortune to run into. Before I was fully aware of it, I was being told that my job was totally satisfactory, and therefore would I submit my final bill? I didn't protest that I hadn't spoken my mind, but gratefully accepted a way out of what was bound to be both futile and embarrassing.

The phenomenon of the corporate conglomerate has given rise to another example of the executive client whose most essential virtue seems also to be his own corporation's major problem.

In an age when ownership often is not expert in the production processes of its own corporation, top management tends to lump an ever increasing number of once disparate functions under an ever decreasing number of business categories. For example, fifty years ago if one corporation produced steam engines and another hydraulic pumps, one corporation would be staffed with experts in steam engines and the other in hydraulic pumps. By today's standards, such an arrangement would seem unnecessary. Since customers who need steam engines are very often the same people who need hydraulic pumps, mightn't one profitably merge both companies and fire one sales force, so that steam engine salesmen also pitched the hydraulic-pump line? In addition to the savings one could make by halving the sales force, many other executives of the acquired company also might be cut back after sharing the wisdom of their industry experience.

This kind of conglomeration of related industrial functions makes sense, even though it seems heartless and leads to the downfall of prerogatives of the acquired company's executives. Of course, the drawbacks are obvious also. If you've been a steam-engine man all your life, it's not likely that you're going to be as good a salesman with the new hydraulic-pump line your company has acquired. This is so not only because of the education you need to acquire, but also because your loyalties will continue to remain primarily with your first business associations. And the intangible trust and long-shared experiences your new customers had with former management are going to be difficult to duplicate regardless of the goodwill involved.

The most recent breed of conglomeration, however, removes takeover management yet another step from an obvious connection with the real functions its acquired companies perform. If a steam-engine and an hydraulic-pump merger would tend to bring together engineers, metallurgists, and salesmen dealing with the same customers, what possible common denominator might an oil company have with a Hollywood movie producer, or a textile mill with a hotel chain?

Modern conglomerate bosses, like the English metaphysical poets of the seventeenth century, "yoke together disparate opposites into new meaningful wholes." But what is the common base? Why does it make sense to put under one umbrella so many different kinds of operations? This is the kind of question once asked by medieval philosophers who wondered what might be the ultimate good toward which nature in its infinite variety and men in their various pursuits all strived. Aquinas put it this way: Ends are more important than means. If a man wants political influence so that he can achieve his sexual designs on the woman of his choice, he obviously wants the woman more than the political influence. If a man wants wealth in order to exert power, his end (power) is a higher goal than the means (wealth). Aquinas wondered if one were to examine all human behavior, what would it be that was sought for its own sake and for which all other desired goals were merely way stations toward the final goal? "Why do you want political power?" "So I can have the woman I want." "Why do you want the woman?" "So that I can win the admiration of all the men in my town." "And why do you want the admiration of these men?" A relentless series of these questions would drive the respondent to say, finally, "Because therein lies happiness." For Aquinas, all human endeavor strove to achieve happiness. What happiness is the happiness toward which all other happinesses strive? he wondered. He would have responded: "The contemplation of God." The modern conglomerate boss would respond, "The maximization of capital."

The inhumanities committed in the name of religion are well known, explainable in terms of a wider scheme to some, damnable on their own face value to others. The inhumanities committed by those other metaphysicians, a particular new breed of conglomerate King, are not as dramatic, but in the calculus of human suffering not inconsequential.

I well remember one man who as a prospective client called me in to talk about his company and his plans. He was one of America's more successful conglomerate magicians. His holdings included savings and trusts, talent agencies, oil companies, real estate, banks, mobile homes, and whatnot. The acorn from which the many-branched conglomerate had sprung was a *Fortune 500* firm, with a long record as a producer of heavy industrial equipment. With each acquisition the conglomerate acquired new personnel. Sometimes trust would be vested in the newly acquired company's historic management. More often than not it was put into the hands of a premier executive who had worked his way up the ladder of the parent company.

The typical procedure would be to take a trusted executive from the parent corporation and make him president of the new acquisition. Not only was he a superior executive—so the rationale went—he also knew the wishes of the Big Boss. In addition, rapport had already been established between them, and the lines of communication—personal as well as formal—had long been in operation.

Admittedly, in some companies such a system of promoting a trusted executive by moving him laterally to another company has many benefits. It gives the excellent vice-president of the parent company a chance to get to the top, whereas if he had stayed in the home base, his career might have topped off. It injects new challenges into the career of an executive who might in the last ten years before retirement become bored by the same old routine. As long as the parent company's major motivation in the operation of the new subsidiary is to run it efficiently at the maximum *reasonable* profit, the conglomerate-acquisition syndrome can be, in rare circumstances, a great benefit to results-oriented senior-level personnel.

In the boom market following the Second World War, however, some opportunistic conglomerate tycoons increasingly began to think of their corporate acquisitions differently: not so much in terms of the products they produced and the profits that might be made from marketing them, but as they did when they initially launched their flagship company at a huge multiple by taking it public the instant it showed a glimmer of sustainable profitability. In short, the product the parent company expected the acquired company to produce was EARNINGS.

Let us assume a parent company started off in the electrical-components business, and after a series of acquisitions was now thinking of acquiring a home-construction company. Were it his company, my prospective client, the *corporate conglomerate King,* would send one of his most trusted operational vice-presidents out to the new subsidiary to become president. At first the new president would be delighted with his status and his newly implemented salary. He would strive to make the home-construction firm the best construction firm in the business.

In order to do so he recommends hiring new personnel, expanding the sales force, upgrading and increasing trade advertising and promotion, modernizing warehousing and inventory control, and computerizing bookkeeping functions. Nobody could sincerely deny that these changes would *in the long run* be of basic importance to the company, both in terms of the quality of performance and the maximization of profit. No one could object to his methods. No one but the accountants from the parent company, that is.

It soon becomes clear that our newly appointed president hadn't understood his job. More nearly correctly, the King hadn't wanted him to understand his job. If he had, the VP would probably have refused it. For the real purpose behind the King's acquisition was not to get into the home-construction business, but to make the new company *seem* as profitable as possible, in the shortest time possible, so that a stock offering could be floated at something like thirty to forty times earnings, and the parent company, in Jimmy Ling fashion, could redeploy its assets. The home-construction company ends up strictly a financial, not an industrial, property; and when companies are considered financial rather than industrial properties, power lies with the accountants, not with the operation executives—not even with the president.

It is not long before the newly appointed president is frustrated, angry, and filled with despair. He doesn't quit, but takes early retirement at fifty-five.

When the King called upon me for recruiting and to offer help in solving a "morale" problem he was having with his division managers, it was not long before I discovered that his tactic was common knowledge among the very best men in the parent organization and that "promotion" to the presidency of a newly acquired subsidiary was a brief joy ride, soon to end in grave disappointment.

The King told me that his best men were accepting jobs with other firms, and despite his protestations that the company's stock was ever climbing, resulting in excellent benefits from their substantial stock options, his most talented men no longer seemed eager to promote the best interest of his corporate empire. What might I suggest? Perhaps a reward-incentive program? Perhaps *more* stock options? What was the cure?

What I couldn't tell the King was that his men had come to see that their professional achievements didn't amount to much in a company which was being operated as a stock-touting combine. Yet I couldn't tell him that the tactic he had used to make for himself and the parent company unheard of profits (perhaps short-lived) was a failure, since earnings per share was the *sine qua non* of his conglomerate ambitions.

The King was too wise a manager not to recognize what his conglomerate acquisitions were doing to his personnel. What he wanted from me was assurance that what he was doing was all right. At my insistence, he would consider some stopgap recommendations which would quiet one executive here, another there, but nothing that would change his essential business strategy. That was set in concrete.

As adroitly as possible, I declined to have anything to do with him. I didn't accept the consultancy and I didn't bill him a cent for my time. Besides the pleasure I got from my apparently altruistic self-denial, I also did myself and some others a favor. The King, and others like him, are death to the really talented, loyal executive. Feeding him worthy candidates who would inevitably be damaged by their association with his kingdom would generate such ill will toward me and my firm that wisdom and valor were, in this case, on the same side.

I'd like to make one more observation about the firm the King managed. Like many others I have run across, it was simply no place for the best people to work. It makes not a jot of difference how successful such companies are: they inevitably destroy the best people. My only advice about these places is to stay away from them, unless you are using them as coldly as they use you: perhaps for some education, perhaps for a brief step up the corporate ladder. The saddest sight in the corporate world is an energetic, loyal, angry young manager trying to change a bad situation which no one in power wants changed. The King has taken his problem to several other headhunters and rehearsed his plight with them as he did with me and others before me. He still hasn't solved his problem. He doesn't want to, but it assuages him a bit to pretend he's trying.

The "idea man" is the bronze Apollo of the executive pantheon. His virtue is the most visible, and when he causes changes, they are the most flashy. Sometimes the idea can change the face of the earth, as did Henry Ford's massive changeover to the production line. Sometimes it is the perception that an obscure scientific development may have immense commercial value, as was John H. Dessauer's recognition of Chester Carlson's then primitive "electrophotography" process—the process which is now known as Xeroxing, and which turned tiny Haloid Corporation into the international business giant Xerox has become. The idea man is in the spotlight, and when he succeeds he is responsible for vast increments in corporate profits. Of course, when he fails, he is liable to commensurate attack, an unsurpassable example of which was Ford's Edsel fiasco. That such blunders result in humiliation and defeat for the executive most closely associated with them may in the hearts of many compassionate people seem unfortunate—certainly no occasion for rejoicing. But even the most softhearted person would have to admit that a corporation which is nearly destroyed by some totally disastrous scheme is justified in trying to excise the most apparent source of the disaster—the executive who started the whole thing in the first place!

While compassion for the idea man whose idea has failed is an understandable human response, it rarely seems necessary. I have noted time and again that when an executive's mistake is grand enough (*i.e.*, expensive and immensely stupid), he is rewarded by his colleagues as if he had succeeded on the same scale as that by which his failure was measured.

Sarnoff's reputation won't be damaged by the colossal failure of RCA's entry into the computer field. Robert McNamara will always be thought of as an organizational genius, despite the fact that his reorganizations destroyed the esprit of much of the military's high-level cadre and that under his heralded cost-benefits system the Alice-in-Wonderland absurdities of the C5A and the TFX were perpetrated. (You may remember that the TFX was the Atomic Age fighter-bomber capable of landing anywhere, even on an aircraft carrier. One of its major drawbacks was that it was so overweight that it threatened to sink any carrier on which it might land.) Howard Hughes is thought of as an industrial genius—but his idea for a super-huge plywood passenger plane cost his company more than 60 million dollars, and for all that, it still hasn't flown more than a few yards at an altitude of a few feet. How many people think that Bernie Cornfeld is anything but a mastermind of the financial community, despite the fact that IOS went bankrupt even more spectacularly than it became Croesus-rich? Any man with the brains to sell mutual funds to Europeans and American servicemen abroad has got to be a genius. Right?

The source of approbation for such notable failures is not difficult to locate. Any executive entrusted with enough power to perpetrate such calamities must be able to make a great impression on other knowledgeable and powerful people. Obviously, only a man of great talent could have been so colossally wrong. The same kind of thinking goes into the epigrammatic observation about personal finances "Your credit is not judged by how much money you have, but by how much money you owe." It's not so much what you do, it's the scale on which you do it.

One of the most morbidly amusing headhunts of which I know (I didn't do it) involved a client's attempts to get rid of the superstar president of his educational publishing and materials subsidiary. This superstar was a super idea man, and it was his long record of startling cerebration that caused the client to hire him in the first place. Looking back over the idea man's record was more educative in retrospect than it must have been in the blinding glow of his first ganglia-crackling interview with the now dissatisfied client.

In the past ten years Mr. Idea had had three senior management jobs. At each corporation he had contributed a notion that had caused a major change. At his first senior management post, Mr. Idea devised a way to sell the firm's least profitable publication through supermarkets. Although he left a year after the plan was put into operation, the results of the new merchandising were highly successful.

With the golden glow of his "great idea" on his record, Mr. Idea went to an electronics firm and started a multimedia electronic study program for educational television and home study. At the end of two years, his second corporation was well on its way to what was to prove a most useful and profitable venture. Our idea man abruptly "resigned."

His third senior management position was with the client's broad-based communications company, which had holdings in radio and television stations, magazines, travel agencies, paper and pulp plants, and book companies. Among his sensational great ideas had been to turn the educational subsidiary into a general-interest book company; to adopt a radical new process for printing book jackets; to dream up a major new encyclopedia project; to develop a new way of using materials from the parent corporation's mass-distribution magazine for one-shot newsstand book-format distribution. Every single one of the ideas was brilliant and, if properly administered, profitable. Every single one was falling flat on its face, and the people in charge of bringing these great ideas to fruition were quitting the corporation in droves or carping so much they had little time to do much else.

In the trade press, at industry seminars and cocktail parties you couldn't go a week without hearing about the brilliance of our super-idea man. He was one of the most respected men in the business—so long as you hadn't worked with him.

The client learned, too late, that his super-executive was so busy coming up with super ideas that he had no time to administer his programs. He was so impressed with himself that he hired lieutenants who were in awe of his super ideas, and who had no rapport with the poor drones who would have to carry them out. He was so sure that his executive time was infinitely valuable that he allowed little or no time for his co-workers to confront him with their problems. And finally, he was so insecure that he thought he had to be brilliant every moment of the day. To be practical, to worry about expense or morale, or about the short-term effects of his plans, threatened his image as super-executive.

The extent of his malfeasance finally reached the client and he decided to get rid of him. But how do you get rid of the man who has become (to the outside world) the most glittering symbol of your corporation's success.

That's what the client wanted the headhunter to do: play a key role in getting rid of the superstar. The client tried to make it seem that his main objective was to find a new executive for the subsidiary and that the headhunter's task was essentially to recruit the right man for the job. But, in truth, even top corporate management was cowed by the monster they had helped nourish.

Their plans for moving the superstar out started with the suggestion that a chairman of the board be created for the subsidiary of which the superstar was president. The chairman would outrank the president, and *he* could fire him. Because the chairman would be drawn from an industry outside the influence of our superstar's reputation, he would have an excuse for not having come under the spell of his sensational past. Upon the superstar's resignation or firing, the chairman would agree to resign "for personal reasons" or some such thing, and a real operational president could step in. Of course, this maneuver required duplicity upon the part of the client and the "chairman." And you might be certain that anyone willing to be hired by a client only to fire a man he doesn't know would likely be an SOB himself.

Into such a hornets' nest only a hornet would venture. Let me give you the incredible bottom line of the story. The bogus chairman arrived on the scene. The superstar president had been told that such a post was being created merely to help him with the long-range planning and general operation of the company. Anybody with reasonable emotional stability would have realized that the sooner he got out the better. But not our idea man. He knew that his ideas were so good that he could defend them to anyone. That he couldn't run his staff or the day-to-day operations of his division probably never occurred to him.

The bogus chairman, a man whom management selected for his reputation as a merciless scoundrel, soon raked the superstar over the coals, but not before he had made it clear that he had gathered incriminating evidence about the superstar from every dissatisfied worker on the superstar's payroll. The chairman had the gall to receive the condemning reports from the superstar's own staff, bypassing the superstar's desk. When the superstar tried to have his "disloyal" workers fired, the chairman overruled him! And still the superstar wouldn't quit.

This ugly, stupid scene ended with the superstar literally in tears, locked in his office, refusing to leave the premises. Only the threat of police action got him out. The police, it seems, had never heard of his sensational business ideas.

Is there any justice? you may wonder. Yes! The bogus chairman, who had agreed to quit after his ax job, became so impressed with himself that he made a power play, and because of the ineptness of his corporate superiors gained control of the publicly held subsidiary. With a different set of faults, he managed to bring the company to its knees in just about the time it would have taken the superstar. Who are the corporate leaders who got themselves into such a state of affairs? It doesn't make much difference any more. A year later they took Chapter Eleven and went bankrupt.

The ability to generate sound and innovative business notions, then, is only one of the skills an executive must have. Because ideas are so satisfying to the man who originates them, they tend to push other business necessities into the background. I think it is doubtful that the functions of executive manager and innovator are compatible. I do not mean to denigrate the managerial function by implying that it is unimaginative, nor the innovative calling by implying that it is impractical. Perhaps what I am denigrating is the world of corporate complexity, which lures the best minds to it with promises that innovation is the role of the executive and the food upon which the future of business will feed, only to present him, when he reaches a position of power, with a work load and an accumulation of ethical hedges and social obligations that make innovation an impractical investment of time and energy, and, more than likely, impossible.

The executives with the best reputation for resourcefulness and the best record of success, at least as far as my knowledge extends, are not innovators—not the Chester Carlsons who invent electrophotography—but recognizers and appliers of other men's flashes of invention—men such as Dessauer and the late Joseph Wilson at Xerox, whose recognition of Carlson's genius paid off only after years of experimentation. Carlson never did another thing for Xerox except clip the millions of dollars' worth of stock certificates he earned, most of which he gave to charity. Wilson and Dessauer successfully went on to lead the company through the day-to-day vicissitudes of business.

Unlike the failure of Mr. Idea, a disappointing development, in a career sense, involved one of the most blameless and highly skilled executives I have ever known, who was the director of internal consulting at a huge firm. The various operations of the firm were highly compartmentalized. Not only were there scores of separate technical and scientific projects going on at the same time, but the firm's various financial services groups were perennially vying with each other to gain budgeting and financial control responsibilities over the many divisions of the company. It was terribly difficult for the managers of one operation to stay in touch with the managers of another; yet, coordination of effort was a critical necessity. If top management of the firm was to allocate funds for the fiscal year wisely, giving priority where priority was needed, it had to have a grasp of what the goals of each one of the divisional projects in the works were, how much they would cost to carry out, and how long they would require to generate profit.

It is easy to understand how each divisional manager will make the strongest possible case for the projects in which his division is involved. In fact, he is *supposed to be a prejudiced advocate* of what he parochially judges the best interests of his division to be. The company-wide view is the responsibility of senior corporate-level management.

Theoretically, parochial advocacy presupposes that each proponent will make the strongest case possible for his project. When all the various pitches from the various departments that are competing for the firm's yearly funds are presented, the top men will then choose the best of the powerfully stated alternatives. In practice there are two serious obstacles to the ideal operation of the method.

First, the parochial advocate finds it difficult to tell his story objectively. Major technical problems tend to become "temporary design flaws soon to be conquered." The high cost of materials for a new hydraulic pump tends to be covered over by a cogent discussion of the savings the new pumping station will afford. The cost of training a new sales team is played down in comparison with the volume of new business the sales force will generate.

The cumulative effect of these minor (and sometimes major) distortions is that top management bases its corporate-level decisions on doctored evidence. And once a division manager gets his fiscal way by having unfairly strengthened his case, he becomes even more set in his ways. The example of his success spurs his managerial peers to compete with him in distorting the evidence.

The other built-in danger of the parochial advocate's method resides with top management. Ideally, each manager should be thought of as an equal of his competing managers. The only basis on which top management should judge his case is the evidence in his presentation. In fact, certain managers tend to accumulate an imbalance of influence just because their previous projects were the ones top management voted to favor. The process is insidious. Because a certain manager successfully argued to allow the new auto battery to be built in his division rather than in a division of his intramural competitors, and because the auto-battery operation was successful, the triumphant manager's fiscal year looks splendid, and his requests for new funds for new projects acquire a not necessarily justified glitter. His new requests for corporate funds may have more influence than they would if they were to be judged solely in comparison with the merits of competing requests.

To make the parochial advocacy method work top management needs a trustworthy report on the specific operations of its complex divisions. This information will most likely not come from a man whose career is strongly identified with any one of the company's operations or groups. What is needed is a generalist who nonetheless has a working knowledge of at least the basic problems of each division, and whose loyalties are primarily to the top and not to the divisions. Yet he must be able to move comfortably between the executive suite and the factory, without appearing to be a corporate fink on one hand or a special pleader for line management on the other.

My executive was just such a man. He had come to work for the firm straight out of college and had performed the most menial tasks. In the course of the next twenty-five years he had worked in almost all the company's divisions, rising slowly and steadily through line management to his present delicate position.

I was appalled when my corporate client asked my opinion on where he could best reassign this executive I had come so much to admire. How could the company be dissatisfied with a man who was doing so crucial a job so well?

Of course I interviewed my old acquaintance, and though habitual loyalty to the company made him reticent, he told me enough to let me know that a line manager had been promoted over his head into a vice-presidency and would assume most of his liaison responsibilities. Not only that, but for the past three years my man had made it known that he felt he deserved a top-level job. Although he had not delivered an ultimatum, he intimated he would not be surprised if his days with the corporation were numbered.

The lessons of this man's case are sad indeed. Because he had made himself indispensable in a certain function, management never thought to move him elsewhere. He couldn't move back to a line manager's role. He had lost the parochiality of vision to plead his case effectively and was concerned that such a move would look like a demotion. Despite a high salary, he hadn't achieved the stature organizationally to be given a seat in the board room and consequently would not have the chance to make policy. His reports to management were looked at as a "service" for decision-makers. Like a lieutenant in a confused battlefield, his walkie-talkie reports from the front line were important, but it was up to the generals to make the important decisions.

Of course, it was my man's *very removal* from advocacy that had made him so vital. Now his objectivity and right-minded subservience to top management had made him seem not enough his own man for the virile policy cadres at the top.

It is naïve to believe that malleability to the desires of management is an unqualified virtue. Without an occasional burst of dissatisfaction or an ill-tempered reluctance to take on yet another difficult assignment without any visible reward, without at least once having considered the offer of employment with another company, the most loyal and talented manager comes to be thought of as too lacking in spunk to be suited for the top-level management. If my man had from time to time been intractable or had forcefully made known his dislike of another manager, I am sure he would have gotten to the executive suite. As things turned out, he was "too nice a guy," "too loyal," "too unambitious" to make a first-rate corporate-level executive, in whom, of course, there must be a leavening of cynicism, self-interest, and ambition.

There is also a particular breed of corporate executive reminiscent of a former client, with whom I have refused further dealings. This kind of man has a reputation for being considerate to his personnel and attentive to their personal needs and ambitions. He is willing to do almost anything for you but give you the kind of unpleasant, corrective advice or admonition that you sometimes need.

His image of himself is that of a wise, battle-tempered veteran who has seen it all, and therefore can appreciate the best in you while tolerating the occasional faults in your character most likely put there by youth, inexperience, or just the lack of opportunity of being trained by the great man himself. While he is being forgiving and praising you for your good job, he is winning your trust and making you feel that if you can satisfy his demands, things will go well with you at the company.

If you have managed to annoy another senior executive by your real or alleged misdeed or inefficiency, you can be sure that our gracious executive will make you feel that you have committed only one of those inevitable errors "which all of us make from time to time, but by which no intelligent person would judge you." He will not arrange a confrontation between you and the colleague you have offended. However, he might risk an unpleasant moment with his peer. If you have been passed over for a raise, he will promise to take your case to the executive suite himself. But he will readily refer it to personnel. If you feel that your talents are not being used in the right way, he will listen to your complaint with immense sympathy and real understanding, assuring you that he'll speak to your supervisor. Instead, what he'll do is ask your supervisor for a report on you and agree with everything your supervisor has said. This kind of executive is so anxious to impress you with his ability to do good things for you that the only thing he will never tell you is that he either doesn't have the power to do them or that your performance is so substandard that you don't deserve having them done for you.

This super-kind executive's psychological objective is to maintain his hold over you by having you think that he is the dispenser of all good things. He is so keen to have your approval that he is afraid to be the bringer of bad news, even when a well-timed remark might be enough to save you from continuing on a path that will lead to your failure. In short, he is a man who not only wants power but also love, and would rather you failed than have you think ill of him. This type is more deadly than the hatchet man. With the hatchet man, at least, you usually get a warning. In his presence you never get complacent. You keep your eyes and ears open to know in what quarters your work has been

judged and what, if anything, was deemed wrong with it.
Through an executive whom I once unsuccessfully tried to recruit for an investment-banking operation, and with whom I stay in touch, not only out of friendship, but because of the value of his acquaintances in the financial world, I learned of a man who incorporated in an almost pure way the poisonous camaraderie of the super-kind executive. My friend had come to know him well, because it was on account of him that he was forced out of his previous job in the investment world.

As is typical of his species, the super-kind executive is a talented man himself. And almost always his virtues are quite flashy. With them he attracts to himself the apparent best of the new young men in the corporation. He has important friends, he travels extensively for the company, his prose style is literate, he has a grasp of sophisticated theory, his conversation is urbane and witty, and even when he discusses day-to-day details he tries to make them illustrate a general point.

When my friend came to the charmer's traditionally conservative firm, he was bent on establishing a reputation as a scrupulously honest fellow who hoped to breathe some new life into the stodgy investment portfolios of the ancient family-trust division. Being young, however, he missed some signs that he was beginning to offend some of the old guard.

His offending actions stemmed from his concern, typical of the investment community in general, with increasing competition of the high-rolling go-go funds and even the more athletic pension and insurance company portfolios. But in his relations with the executive charmer he was constantly reassured that his drive to find new investment opportunities was welcome and that his vigorous new thinking was just what the firm needed.

Encouraged by his boss, my friend concentrated more and more on seeking out new areas for investment. He wrote an unsolicited study in his spare time on the poor performance of motors stocks and the decreasing profitability of certain steels. His initiative was praised. The reports were deemed excellent and eloquent. At least that is what our executive charmer led our young man to believe.

When he had first come to the firm, a fair share of his buy and sell suggestions had been followed. Now, after two years, his suggestions were almost invariably turned down. Whereas formerly he had often met with the senior investment executives to discuss the reasons behind their decisions, and whereas senior officers had come to him for his opinion, he was now almost completely frozen out, left alone to do his job in isolation. He was passed over for raises twice. Finally our executive charmer had a confidential talk with him, telling him that he was too talented for the firm, that there was some inscrutable force which was keeping him from getting to where he belonged, and that it would be in the young man's best interests to find work elsewhere. It was only because our executive was such a good friend of the young man that he told him this unpleasant truth—that's what he claimed, at least.

In a small corporation, there is usually no room for the charming confidence man. His record of unfulfilled promises finally alienates enough of the working staff so that management can read his hollow record clearly. It is in major corporations that he is most often found. His power comes from his ability to charm the inner sanctum of senior-level corporate executives, who are snowed by his exterior but are rarely in a position to measure his daily nonperformance.

His magnanimity in praising his colleagues, his ability to make wise business generalizations from disparate facts, his habit of searching for a lesson in the specifics, impresses the bosses. He tries to appear to have no time for the petty, the trite, the mundane details of ordinary business.

Because he recognizes that the source of his power lies

in his gracious appearance in the eyes of the board, it is this graciousness that he insists on bringing into his contacts with his staff. The trouble is that in nine out of ten instances the problems his staff is experiencing are anything but grand, are resistant to elegant solutions, and do not make good excuses for wise discourse.

While the charmer was encouraging my young investment banker to think big and suggest change, what he didn't mention was the truculent reluctance on the part of senior investment management to change anything at all. What he didn't mention was that our young man's Mormon upbringing probably excluded him from a shot at the top. He also didn't mention that, in any confrontation between top management and our charmer, our charmer would retreat from justifying the actions of the young man immediately. He also found it too unpleasant to mention that the steel and motors investments the young man had advised against were positions originally taken and increased by the retired vice-president for investments, who now was no less a personage than the chairman of the board.

If our young man had been energetically and persuasively represented by our charmer, he might have come through nobly. But the risk was too much for the charmer's courage, and at the first sign of discontent with our young man's aggressiveness he lapsed into opaque platitudinous wisdom. He probably said something like this: "You've got a point, Mr. Chairman, and to tell you the truth, despite how much I admire the young man's intelligence in some matters, I've always found him a bit precipitous. A lot of fellows these days think that there's a way to instant wisdom in the investment game. Well, we know that's a long way from the truth. I think I can drum some sense into his head. If I can't—well, you know, it will be hard, but we'll have to send him packing."

Beware charm without abrasion. Nietzsche, when he was thinking of what it was that he most disliked in the Christian ethic, concluded that it was its tendency to delay the cure by applying an immediate balm that provided only temporary relief. It delayed the permanent remedy which could be achieved only by pain. The parable he concocted is that of the man with a crooked leg. The Christian offers the man a crutch. The Nietzschean moral man breaks the man's leg in order to reset it. The Christian cure results in a man with a permanent disability, who limps around on a crutch. The harsh Nietzschean ethic results in a man who has two sound legs.

The wise executive on the corporate make will always wonder what it is that a senior executive who is seemingly befriending him can do for him. I would advise the young executive to value specific favors a lot more than impressive speeches. The executive charmer can tempt you into indiscretions you would never have dreamed of committing unless you had been entrapped by his bogus votes of confidence. Your best protection from him is to put a high priority on corrective criticism. If you discover that your so-called allies sympathize with you after you've made mistakes, but never offer criticism in advance of making them, you have a good reason to become cynical about the value of their advice, and perhaps even the strength of their character.

A subspecies of executive I have found among my clients, whose virtues you must fear more than his faults, is the man who has not learned the meaning of Jesus' statement that "the poor are always with us." So determinedly democratic (leveling) is he that clod and genius alike receive equivalent justice from his corporate bench. More often than not, the result of such treatment is that the clods are loyal and immensely grateful while the geniuses are resentful and quick to accept other offers of employment.

By refusing to make special cases for special employees, an executive often establishes a reputation for admirable disinterest when he should be castigated for his reluctance to make judgments on character and talent essential to molding a good staff. He often seeks a modest level of intelligence and ambition, because higher levels threaten by comparison to dramatize his own weakness.

I can think of two firms, one a giant in publishing, the other a billion-dollar computer company, which have achieved remarkable reputations for the longevity of their personnel. I found it curious, however, that in their respective industries a remarkably large share of their competitors' top executives had at some time in the past worked for these loyalty-building firms. Doubly remarkable was that these men, once you started to make a list of them, were way above average; in fact, the alumni were a lot more distinguished than the true-blue loyalists from whose ranks they had been recruited.

Both of the superloyal companies shared some essential similarities. They were still controlled by the original owners; both had the corner on a product or marketing system which had originally made for their success and which still was producing well. At the heads of these firms sat elderly managers, whose loyalties lay with established friendships and whose business strategies were never more inventive than necessary to make the old system stand up.

It is almost inevitable that these firms seek managers who want to level out talent and individuality. And the kinds of men who do that best, in order to disguise their motives, parry the demands talent makes, making it go through all the excruciating hurdles of corporate checks and balances, delays, autocratic committee meetings, promotions by seniority, vacations by company tenure, the automatic subjugation of intuitive to the statistical, the discouragement of initiative by restricting job definitions, the requirement that brilliant notions be passed up a line of dullards, and so on *ad nauseum*.

A candidate whom I successfully placed at the very top of an advertising agency described how the firm he had just left had been mediocritized (also, I am sorry to report, made increasingly profitable) by a very attractive and skillful executive leveler.

For years the firm had produced the cleverest, least orthodox, honest, witty campaigns. The place was dripping with inventiveness; the creative department were the stars of the operation. The founder of the firm and the most brilliant creative mind in the place had built the company to nourish Creative. But then the old man died.

The new president was a Harvard Business School type who had recently been a vice-president of marketing for a profitable "slide rule" consumer packaged-goods company. Cost accountants were asked to drill copywriters in the benefits of good financial planning; copywriters lectured on what makes a good ad to traffic managers and account executives; creative chiefs were required to attend outside market-research seminars regularly and to wade through the statistical read-outs of computerized consumer-preference questionnaires, thereby robbing them and their clients of time that could have been spent on creative projects.

Invariably it was the creative types who balked at the structured regime of marketing; invariably agency management thought account executives and creative people should exchange functions to some extent and, in effect, become more alike. The new boss thought he could treat artists and artisans alike. He was wrong, and as more "solid" information was programmed into the artists, the less artistic and imaginative their ads became. A wholesale firing in Creative was the result. A new, malleable cast was recruited, one willing to create to order.

The new staff is doing beautifully, creating ads almost as successful as the one in which Mr. Whipple squeezes the Charmin or the one in which the little A's fight a losing battle for gastric suzerainty against the B's. All that's been lost is respect for the viewer's intelligence; either that or the viewer's intelligence itself. I choose to believe the former.

If you intend to succeed because of your differences from the crowd instead of because of your similarity to it, beware the corporate leveler. You'll be leveled right out of a job.

The last deadly virtue I have noticed among my celebrated corporate clients is the company president I call the Reorganization Man. His art is to institute an endless series of structural innovations which create absolutely no change of substance. His handiest tool is a constantly circulating supply of the same relatively quiescent mediocrities whose low level of achievement was responsible in the first place for the Reorganization Man's notion that it was restructuring time again.

An often stated motive behind an upcoming change is the Reorganization Man's desire to "increase interdepartmental communication." An assistant sales manager may become attached to product development, so that only products with above-average sales potential are given serious attention. The trouble with the plan is that the assistant sales manager often becomes available for reassignment when it is apparent that he is going nowhere in the sales department anyway. As unsuited as he is to the department in which he was trained and supposedly intimately knowledgeable, he is even less suited to a department about which he knows nothing and where he has few friends. What's more, the reason the mediocre assistant sales manager has been kept on as long as he has is that his boss, the vice-president of sales, couldn't attract good men to his department because he himself had long since stopped fighting the company's lethargy. He had learned that the inertia was too potent to countervail. The newly transplanted assistant sales manager, therefore, now reports to a marketing vice-president who is convinced that nothing intelligent can come from him. Even if by accident a bright idea should push up through the muck, the marketing vice-president recognizes that no one else in the organization would know how to distinguish it from the same old you-know-what.

Another favorite reorganization of our Reorganization Man is to get the boys in the executive suite back "in touch" with the geographically dispersed divisions. Our Reorganization Man feels that there has been a loss of contact between top management and the day-to-day operations of the company. He wants, therefore, that his most trusted cronies monitor and participate in functions which seem to have come loose from the headquarters executives, who originally delegated their jurisdiction.

For such a situation to work, the monitoring executive must be familiar with the operations of the division on which he has been sent to check. He must also respect the prerogatives and handle carefully the pride of the present line management. He must be able to report his findings directly to the top, candidly and promptly. Even then, it would take the most intelligent and socially adroit executive to get the information he wants without destroying the morale of the division into which he has intruded his authority.

In the typical futile exercise of such a reorganization plan, at least one of several things dooms it from the start. The essential problem is that the trouble lies not with the divisions but with the executive suite. Cronyism and the laziness caused by unearned security and excess luxury may have made the corporate headquarters the last place to find executive talent. If, in fact, there is a chronic problem in line management, the fact that it is *chronic* shows that the fault lies at the top, from which eminent corrective directives or direct personal intervention should long ago have cured the situation. Since, however, these cures were not forthcoming, the divisions have developed an intramural corruption of their own, mimicking the lofty incompetence of their executive progenitors.

In short, no amount of rearranging beer glasses is going to produce champagne.

Once one sees through the hoax which the Reorganization Man is intentionally or unintentionally perpetrating by his apparently deeply thought out blueprinted shuffles, it is either appalling or amusing to see the praise he wins for his initiative. Because of their constant needs for new personnel, several of my clients have been Reorganization Men. They are "man-eaters." In such circumstances, my candidates qualify by their mediocrity or cynicism. Because on such headhunts one satisfies the client by allowing him to agitate only the surface of his stagnant pond, his respect for the job I have done is in direct proportion to how little of importance I have accomplished.

If a corporation executive sees himself, or a part of himself, in these portraits of clients for whom it is almost impossible for a headhunter to do a good job, I hope the recognition can be educative. For any corporate client who throws his money away is foolish and should learn to resent paying my fee.

A client should know how much a headhunter is going to cost him. I find few things more irritating than the client who made me bill him repeatedly after I found him the superstar he wanted because he had discovered he would have to pay at least $10,000 more than he expected. When I showed him the considerably lesser person he could get for what he wanted to pay, after a display of deriding him, he showed his colors by offering him the job. When he called me six months later, on another search, we started the whole damned process over again, late payment and all.

When figuring what a headhunt will cost, the client should

not think that he is paying only my fee. He has to build into his calculations what he will have to pay if I come up with the kind of excellent manager he claims he wants.

Bad clients come in many guises. One of my clients in the Southwest misuses me by turning to me for what amounts to miracles. A large company, and quite successful at that, they simply are not in the real world on executive salaries. They know they can't through their own efforts come up with the quality executives they seek for the money they pay. They come to me for that. Their purpose is not to find the best man to do a classy job, but to get me to find the proverbial needle in the haystack who will fit with their niggardly salary structure.

They are, in company form, what the anthropologist calls *ethnocentric*. The top management thinks their corporate "culture" is something special and incoming executives are lucky to have the opportunity to practice their craft under their roof. The executive vice-president told me once (after failing to attract the best candidate I was able to present on a search for a general sales manager because the company and the candidate were $2,500 apart), "Out here in the West, we enjoy life. We think there is more to it than a big salary. We enjoy our work for more than just economic gain. A man in order to get ahead should be willing to make a lateral or even a backward move on money." I agree that in exceptional cases this is good advice, but in that company, such thinking is a rationalization for damaging niggardliness.

Of course, when I accept a search assignment from these people I begin with one hand tied behind my back. Naturally, I don't attempt to go after the best man because the company is adamant and inflexible in its compensation program and I would only be wasting a good man's time as well as my own. So while this client tells me he "wants the best" he never sees the best because I will not use my time so foolishly. Every search I have concluded with this company, except one, has resulted in the placement of a mediocre candidate—one they could "afford."

A bad client is someone who pays a lot of money in fees but refuses to meet with certain candidates I recommend. If he knows something about the man that I don't, he should tell me what it is and I can learn something. If he doesn't know something more than I do, he should see the candidate or fire me.

Along this line, I often hear clients say to me, "I don't want to see your candidate from XYZ Company because nobody over there can be any good." Clients often fail to realize that the best candidates in middle management often come from poorly managed, poorly organized companies, because an aggressive, inner-directed manager is thrown into a broader range of problems in a company where problems are a way of life and management is incompetent.

A bad client is a man who wants "pretty" candidates. For him, all I need to do is package a handsome man, six feet tall, holder of any Ivy League degree, preferably a Harvard or Wharton MBA. He should be well-tailored, and, as David Riesman says, have a wife who is "of the station wagon variety."

An amusing spoof of the attractive-only, executive-profiled, prestigiously educated candidate appeared over a year ago in a blind ad in *The Wall Street Journal:*

POSITIONS AVAILABLE

MAYBE . . .

. . . you're the right guy. Here's a different kind of opportunity for a different sort of person. Bear with us. We are the principal owners of a loosely-knit, smallish, but highly-promising group of companies. Total sales in 1972 may hit $10 million, possibly a good bit more. Our aims and potential are far greater. We are essentially entrepreneurs

who like to put things together. But we're
not inclined toward the operating side, and
we need the right guy to run our burgeoning
enterprise. The components are not strictly
related and everything at the moment does
not fit into neat little compartments. We
have an incredibly promising computer-
related electronics company which isn't yet
off the ground, even though the world is
waiting for the patented products we've got
for sale. We have a leisure-oriented, retail-
wholesale company which ought to be
expanded. We have an old-line snack food
manufacturer which can be the nucleus for
a much-larger operation. We are close to
acquiring a couple of other interesting companies. But, as we said, our operations are
loosely-run and crying for good, tough day-
to-day management. Somewhere the right
guy exists. Maybe you're the one! We're
mildly prejudiced against Harvard MBAs,
which won't rule you out entirely. But having a Harvard MBA won't give you a leg
up on other candidates. We want a solid,
shirt-sleeve type who can shape up our
individual companies, build sound organizations, get maximum mileage out of a buck,
turn a good profit, and move toward achieving the obvious potential in each separate
company. If you sell us, we'll give you
plenty of rope. We won't hold your age
against you, young or older. You don't have
to be witty or dapper or 6'3" with an executive profile. We merely expect you to get
the job done. While we like to think we're
at least mildly "with it," we do lean to such
musty virtues as loyalty and dependability.
You'll probably need a sense of humor. If
you panic when money's tight, forget us,
because we're undercapitalized and employment with us could be injurious to your
health. But if you've read this far, think
you've got what we're looking for, and are
hungering for a stiff challenge like this,
here's what we will offer the right guy: (1)

a good base salary: (2) a real opportunity to make a lot more if you produce: (3) a shot at a meaningful piece of equity which we hope will make you rich: (4) reasonably generous benefits which fall way short of IBM: and (5) a good many headaches and hassles until you get a handle on things. If you're the right guy, you'll probably answer this ad. (Maybe somebody will send it to you in case you miss it.) If you're not the right guy, you're already convinced we're beneath your dignity or just kidding. If you do reply, give us the full story on yourself right off the bat—everything! Oh, yes, we're based in Chicago, which we think is the world's No. 1 city for business. Address your reply to: Owners,

Box CX-854, The Wall Street Journal.

A bad client is a man who thinks he can do reference checks better than I can and gets a candidate fired from his current job by poking around indiscreetly. One such client stupidly called the employers of two non-job-seeking executives (the executives, of course, had not told their bosses that they were looking at another opportunity) and put the future of those men in question.

A bad client is a man who shows a candidate's references to him or quotes from them. This is particularly unethical because I secure references by giving solid assurances to the parties offering the information that it will be used with complete discretion by me and my client only.

A bad client is a man who tells me he is in a great hurry to hire an executive to solve an urgent problem, and then postpones seeing my candidates for a month after I unearth them.

Some ingenious but short-sighted clients, seeking immunity from corporate raiding, like to divvy up various search assignments between search firms so that the firms, knowing that the company is a client, will never recruit from them. One client, apparently not aware of the ethical standards of our profession, sent me a contract for signature in which I was to agree not to recruit *from* them in the future. This was *while* I was doing an assignment for them. I sidestepped the issue as diplomatically as possible until I completed the assignment. This was an insult to me. I would never recruit from a client, nor would any headhunter with half a brain, ethics aside.

Another client, without my knowledge, had me, along with two other search firms, working on the same search. What a total bill they must have received from the three of us! Had we known, we would not have been party to such a silly situation.

Despite my various contacts in the corporate world, I've never met the unflawed executive, the man described in this anonymous poem, with which it is perhaps appropriate to assuage corporate executives who think my reciting their various flaws is an indication that I expect an unreal perfection.

> From what I've read in magazines
> And seen in sundry movie scenes,
> The true executive is he
> Who delegates authority,
> Who resolutely, firmly acts,
> But only when he has the facts,
> Who speaks well, writes a splendid letter,
> But also listens even better,
> Who cares about his men, their wives,
> But doesn't meddle in their lives,
> Who knows details, yet keeps his eye
> On goals beyond minutiae,
> Who works as long as anyone,
> And leaves his desk clear, tasks all done,
> Who keeps his word, although it hurts,

Who never drinks too much, or flirts,
Who even on the darkest days
Can summon up a word of praise
And bravely smile amidst disaster,
Who goes to church, and knows the pastor,
Who chairmans P.T.A. and Chest,
Who, hale and hearty, needs no rest,
But is, of course, a sportsman too,
Topnotch with golf club, gun, canoe,
The true executive, in short,
Is good at work and good at sport,
Resourceful, charming, man of talents,
Possessed of perfect poise and balance.
His words and deeds and aims all mesh . . .
I'd like to see one in the flesh.

V. THE SYSTEM

America had the potential to become a land of abundance and that her working men and business pioneers made that promise of abundance fact is one of the most impressive achievements in history.

Yet now for the first time in history, the automatic equation of abundance with beneficence is not always made. Business leaders are being forced to recognize the double edge a significant proportion of the present generation of Americans puts on the concept of abundance. There is a strong antigrowth philosophy among them which only ignorant businessmen can dismiss as youthful and frivolous. This philosophy embraces matters of environmental and social reengineering which its adherents deny can be achieved by corporations operating as they have in the past. And the beliefs involved in such viewpoints are not going to dissolve as these young people grow older.

The argument of the antigrowth philosophy is not merely economic, aimed at the effects of an expanding economy on the earth's finite resources. It goes deeper than that. The *spiritual* side of the antigrowth attack maintains that the ideology of abundance and growth is not improving the quality of life for the citizen, but corroding it. With the adherents of the social protest movement I espouse many things in common. Their recognition of urgent, material, social and spiritual problems and their sharp, insistent pamphleteering in which they both single-out villains and suggest remedies, has done much to spur a too often quiescent business and federal establishment. But I, as a firmly entrenched and supportive member of the business community, see in the just mandates for change directed at us, not a herald of our demise, but a challenge, which if met imaginatively, can only improve the quality of life for all citizens, and make the business of business even more deeply satisfying. The corporate headhunter, I believe, can be right at the red-hot center as an instrument in helping bring about some of these changes.

Absolutely no one can dispute that the paradigm of the new corporate leader is changing. In the past, if profits were up, shareholders were happy. When a chief executive retired, and he and the board had been doing their jobs, the scenario called for the new man to continue with business as usual. Today the men who have been groomed to succeed the retiring chieftans will not only be operating in a different economic climate from their predecessors.

. . . They will be grappling with issues that were once peripheral: pollution control, minority-hiring practices, consumerism, and women's liberation. Moreover, they will be challenged to demonstrate that continuing economic growth is indeed desirable. Keeping pace with technology will exacerbate the pressures. In brief, the priorities have drastically changed from the time their predecessors were elevated to the top job.[1]

[1] "Old Bosses Bequeath New Problems," *Business Week,* January 1, 1972, p. 50.

In the search for the men to function successfully in the new environment in which corporate business will be conducted, the headhunter has to be acquainted with the new breed of executive-level businessman whose sensitivities and training have brought him into contact with critical elements of society and government which traditionally have been thought of as anti-business. Perhaps, more importantly, the headhunters chosen by exciting, responsible companies will be those who have the insight to ascertain who, among the current crop of middle management, not formally trained or exposed to the new attitudes, have the capacity and motivation to assume more socially responsive roles in American business. The delicate task of the new executive will be to show understanding and sympathy towards critics of industry while maintaining the trust of his corporate colleagues and shareholders. He will eschew impressive but empty rhetoric from a socially conscious homiletical grab bag, and urge his company to act in the national interest while promoting those profit-taking aspects of his operations which are productive of permanent human good.

An example of one new kind of corporate executive I think we headhunters increasingly will be asked to uncover is a sort of in-house, humanistic ombudsman. For lack of a completely accurate title, he could be called Vice-president of Corporate Responsibility.

It could be argued, of course, that this job should be absorbed in the responsibilities of the president. In some companies and by some presidents this would undoubtedly be the case. But on a broad scale, it is unlikely that most presidents' ambitions, which got them to the pinnacle of their companies, would permit them to give the attention to this job that it requires. Personally, I would exult in recruiting distinguished men and women for some of the country's greatest and most resourceful corporations who make a hardheaded commitment to such a purposeful undertaking.

Because in most cases the president cannot attend properly to such duties, it is essential that the vice-president of corporate responsibility report directly to the president. To do his job, he must have the top man's support. His opinions, public statements and actual authority will offend many less altruistic managers who will be sniping at him and working resourcefully to bring about his downfall. As the voice of conscience of the company, he serves as an in-house humanistic critic in command of corporate operating information. Unlike well-meaning but often uninformed outside critics, he will be knowledgeable at first hand, without such intermediaries as irresponsible third parties or flap-happy corporate public-relations flaks.

It is crucial that the vice-president of corporate responsibility not be conceived as a glorified director of public and community relations. Nor can he be a cocktail-party liberal who flippantly derides corporate ways, prattling in a fog, naive about the demands of corporate machinery and means of decision making. He must believe in the profit motive, and that corporations are the major engines providing citizens with goods and services and the vehicles for greater human potentialities. He must have a sense of indignation that will be aroused when he sees the corporation abdicating or corrupting that role, and must believe that in intelligent reform the system returns to its proper and efficient function. He, from inside, should outdo the demands of HEW, EPA, EEOC, FEPC, and beat them at their own game.

He should make sure the company is hiring enough minority workers; he should set up a counseling and referral service for employees having problems with alcoholism, with children on drugs, or otherwise hopelessly in trouble. He should see that all employees have access to adequate medical care, and look to see what minority businesses can be backed. He must take an adamant and knowledgeable stand against the expansion of ecologically damaging processes, and make suggestions aimed at phasing out such operations and sub-stituting other profitable but sane ones. He should be con-cerned with job enrichment, communications in both direc-tions between labor and decision makers, and be more innovative in defending the interests of the company's work-ers than the union.

He should encourage new life styles in his company, or at least not allow the stifling of such at the hands of the traditional rep-tie, brown-shoe group. And it is absolutely necessary that he serve on the board of directors.

This is all terribly idealistic, I know. But I also know that its advent in one form or another is inevitable. Conditions require it. Some firms, no matter how haltingly, are already attempting the enactment of such a job concept. More and more companies will be seeking men who can breathe life into the concept. These are the companies with which I want to work.

In traditional economic thinking it is the availability of physical resources that determines the kind of jobs available to the labor market. If oil is available, there is a need for oil men; if wheat can be grown, a need for wheat farmers, and so on. In short, it is the availability of the physical resource that creates the demand for the human resource. In America, all that is changing, and, in fact, has already drastically changed.

Through the instruments of widespread higher education and a populace freed by the blessings of economic abundance, we have a highly skilled work force which more and more refuses to work at tasks it finds demeaning. More people demand jobs commensurate with their notion of what industry should be doing *for* America and not *to* it. In ever increasing numbers, college-educated youth and enlightened managers of traditional corporations are creating a talent pool which has become its own natural resource. The availability of human talent, just as the availability of coal or iron, will create industries which can make use of its potential. Instead of starting with the physical resource, however, industry will start with the human resource. This is what is behind the unprecedented growth of the service industries.

I believe that the level of talent and social responsibility among corporate executives will soar in the next decade. Corporations need good men and good men won't work for corporations who offend their sense of what's right. It is in this cyclical reinforcing of talent and corporate responsibility that the excitement of the near future lies for us headhunters.

But one does not have to look only to the future to see why the demand for greater excellence at the top is increasing. The years of America's unchallenged economic dominance are gone, and long periods of spectacular boom seem unlikely. Under these conditions only the sleek survive.

However, apart from any of the objective pressures on industry from Government regulation and foreign competition, or from ecological critics or shareholders, there is a psychological or spiritual change which is affecting the ways employees think about their careers.

I find it fascinating that the word *career* did not assume its connection with the kind of work a man did until the nineteenth century. When the word entered the language in the seventeenth century, it described a racing enclosure for horses. A related word is "careen." A word that described the careening, galloping all-or-nothing quality of a race horse became appropriate in the nineteenth century to describe a man's lifelong job. Obviously there is in the nineteenth-century notion of work, then, the assumption of tremendous aggressiveness and competition in which all the rewards go to the man who fights the hardest. This traditional notion of career is under attack in our country.

The January 19th, 1971, issue of *The Wall Street Journal* contained a front-page article called "The Great Escape."

It documented some of our nation's more affluent adults quitting the corporate world to lead simpler lives. Not one of the men *The Journal* interviewed was a failure in the business world, but for one reason or another, each felt that corporate life was keeping him from an essential fulfillment. The dominant theme of dissatisfaction is strongly antiurban, and those dropout executives who move into the country often take up organic gardening. They make the contrast between the pollution of the city, the "yellow cast of the sky," and what they are presently doing. One executive, in fact, sums up his present defection as a struggle against *contamination*.

Obviously "contamination" is being used both literally and metaphorically. It is important not to overlook the literal meaning before going on to more abstract meanings. When William Blake was thinking of a visual image to condemn the industrial hells of the eighteenth century in England he chose "those dark Satanic mills." Dickens, at his most socially inflamed, paints unforgettable pictures of the dark, dank, and filthy city. The modern city is the city made possible by industry, and whether or not manufacturing is actually carried on in it, the city has come to stand for the worst sins of industrial America.

There was a popular genre of nineteenth-century fiction which might be called "the young man from the provinces" tale. In these works, a country lad, innocent but intelligent and energetic, comes to the city, where first he is duped by the sharpies, but where later he beats them at their own game. He has become successful, but he is still possessed of his original rural virtue. We are made to feel that with men like him in control, the engines of power and influence will soon be producing good.

Just try to imagine writing such a novel today. If anybody is moving anywhere it is out of the city. The headmaster of the grade school our daughter attends, which is located near downtown Chicago, tells me of the renewed trend on the part of city parents to move to the suburbs. The only people we can imagine coming into the heart of the city with a strong desire for change and a close relationship to its citizens are militant radicals. The city, then, is a central metaphor as well as a distasteful reality in the lives of the executive dropout.

Another theme in the list of executive dissatisfactions is that in business they had no self-generated concept of themselves. One executive cites the ethic of accumulating money with no other aim than accumulation. Another refers to the impossibility of community involvement when one is spending four hours a day commuting between the suburbs and the city, and others state that while living in the city they could never be alone, or while living in suburbia, their only company was children who didn't understand their aims.

These men found that geography, time, and the very goals for which they worked (money and prestige) were conspiring to cut themselves off from themselves, and they took remedies. John Koehne, after more than twenty years of working as a highly paid CIA analyst, drives a pickup camper truck decorated with peace symbols. Jim Benton, thirty-five, a former industrial engineer, plans to buy a remote piece of land in New England and work it with his own hands. John Thompson, forty-seven, a former dentist, is preparing to set sail for the high seas at the helm of *Brigadoon II,* a battered 100-ton freighter that is his family's new home. Edward Johnson, sixty, who was once director of employee relations at United Airlines in Chicago, works in Colorado as a toolmaker at a fraction of his former salary. Ross Denver, fifty-two, quit a $50,000-a-year job as head of Amsted Industries Inc.'s research department to till a cranberry bog in Three Lakes, Wisconsin.

These men for the most part were not converted by friends; they simply had had enough. What is most interesting is many are working as hard or harder at this juncture in their lives than ever before.

Herman Rottenberg labored at building a successful sweater-manufacturing firm for twenty-seven years. Now he has a $1-dollar-a-year "job" teaching international folk dancing and running a folk dance magazine. He says he has the old drive in him from business days—only this time it isn't applied to making money. He says, "In business I was thrown in with people who made a lot of money and had as their life's goal acquiring more of it. The more I saw of these people, the more anxious I was not to become one of them."

Tony Rousellot, thirty-five, was for eleven years a broker on the floor of the New York Stock Exchange. He and his wife and two children have taken up residence among the Indians, Chicanos and hippies of Taos, New Mexico. He says he isn't averse to going back into business "if it means running a canning plant for organic vegetables. But it has to be worthwhile. And I'm going to be nobody's employee." Looking back on his career he says that there is "one great advantage about working in the New York Stock Exchange: It gives you absolutely no talent for anything else. So now I have total freedom to do whatever I think is meaningful."

That modern corporate careers tend to so fill a man's life that he is made unfit for all other kinds of work is a common complaint among the executive defectors. Brown Bergen, thirty-five, former insurance salesman and computer-systems analyst, says, "If you give most of your waking hours to a company, they own you. . . . Doing the same thing every day for decades is deadening."

Dissatisfaction with corporate life is a well-publicized fact among the young; it is not so well known among those men who in years past would probably have moved rather predictably to the top of the corporate ladder.

Eugene E. Jennings, professor of management at Michigan State's graduate school of business administration and an authority on executive behavior has said the traditional belief that once an executive gets deep roots in a company he develops a sense of himself which provides permanent justification for his life is disappearing. Jennings believes that the corporation is now running into a group of relatively young executives who were raised on so many options that a straight career path is inimical to their characters.

In a survey made between 1965 and 1970 of some 1,900 corporate vice-presidents and presidents, 205 of them left their offices before mandatory retirement age. That compares with no more than 8 percent who left before mandatory retirement between 1948 and 1953.

Remarking on this phenomenon of early retirement in *The Wall Street Journal,* Eric Morgenthaler concludes that a cherished axiom of corporate success is being challenged: that the rewards at the top of the ladder are so great that men will stay there as long as they can. The lament of Douglas J. Dayton, forty-six, who last year resigned as senior vice-president of Dayton-Hudson Corporation is typical: "I couldn't look forward to anything much different. There was enough change going on in the world that I decided I'd like to sit back and assess it, which I couldn't do on the job."

Critics of the corporate way of life find it easy to explain the dissatisfaction of a growing number of executives within the corporation. Impersonality, money for the sake of sheer accumulation, environmental villainy, hypocritical ethics, disassociation from spirituality, lack of social conscience, concentration on minute tasks that disassociate the individual from a coherent picture of life: these are the indictments which men who leave the corporation most often make.

That the disaffected executive feels this way is undeniable, and that the qualities of unity, meaning, spirituality, inwardness, closeness to nature, and self-reliance are missing in the corporation is true. What I find most interesting and perhaps most pernicious, is that Americans have increasingly come to look to the corporation for kinds of fulfillment one thought it proper to seek in religion, love of family, country and self. And, so while it is legitimate to point to the corporation for its failures, it is blindness not to see that the reason the corporation has come to symbolize our alienation is that our other institutions have failed to provide fulfillment.

I have no intention of analyzing the causes of these breakdowns in our society. Did the corporation with its attendant bureaucracy produce the society in which interpersonal cohesion was lost? I don't know, but would love to hear that point debated by sociologists and historians with more competence than I. What I feel I can say, and say with moral conviction and downright pragmatism, is that since the corporation is being looked to for both blame and remedy, no matter what the corporate world thinks about this justification for the attention, it cannot evade doing something about it.

Apart from moral obligations to ensure the quality of life in America and the moral and emotional well-being of our citizens, executives are being forced to recognize that the corporation has little choice in being sought for cures for national maladies. Power breeds responsibility, or at least it makes those who suffer the burdens of our troubled times look to the seats of power for remedies. There are only two places in this country where power of the magnitude requisite for massive renascence exists: one is the Government, the other is industry. The citizenry is with every passing day demanding more vocally and more impatiently that these two repositories of power act on the behalf of the people. And I fear that continued refusal to agree or acquiesce in significant pleas for change will destroy the consent of the governed.

If people are blaming the corporation for the death of the

inner city, it won't help corporations to document the multiplicity of causes which led to their decay, and of which the corporation is only a part. If the urban corporation is to attract the best work force, it has to lead the way in the cities, regardless of what it believes to be its moral share of the burden.

If executives find their jobs stultifying because they feel cut off from events in the outer world, it will do no good to claim that the corporation can only be responsible for its own operations. Programs will have to be found to involve executives in the community work from which they find themselves estranged.

Admittedly, some of the reasons executives are copping out are not justified. Further, that they blame the corporation for not being able to meet their needs may reflect a simplistic world view and design for living. After all, the last thing needed by the starving peoples of the world is for the better minds of business to go into organic farming. The end result is the same, however, and reflects a trend: abandonment of the corporation and hostility to its ways. There are moral and practical reasons for corporations to keep their most intelligent and sensitive employees, the ones who are most cognizant of the present malaise of American corporate life.

One issue to which headhunters and management experts of every kind can constructively address themselves is the liberation of energy from executives who operate at about 20 percent of capacity despite their cries that they get to the office at 7 A.M. and don't get home until 9 that night. They are not lying about their hours, for the most part. They are unaware, however, of the appalling waste of intelligence and dedication that their corporate duties entail.

A prime leech on corporate efficiency and morale is "luxury," which Robert Townsend, the witty author of *Up the Organization,* describes in a talk delivered before the

Center for the Study of Democratic Institutions' symposium on "The Corporation and the Quality of Life."

Townsend downplays the part that large salaries play in the evils generated by "luxury." Instead he pinpoints a more subtle and a deadly effect: insulation; the loss of eyeball-to-eyeball contact with the people and the specific problems they are charged with handling.

In the typical Townsend scenario, a youthful intelligent hotshot is hired by top management, and he is so impressive that no one would be at all surprised if he wound up in the highest echelons of management. In the beginning of his career, no job is too menial for him. If, for example, his secretary's electric typewriter breaks down, and the office manager is slow in replacing it, he goes down the hall and personally learns just what the problem is. Coincidentally he learns something about how the physical necessities of the office are provided. He has also made an impression on his secretary and convinced the boys in the supply office that when Mr. Youthful asks for something, you'd better give it to him quick.

If the accounting department is slow in getting out checks to a good supplier of his, he doesn't refer the matter to an assistant or write a memorandum to a vice-president which chronicles the problem so that the files may be aware of it. What he does do is pick up the phone and say that he needs the check right away and he volunteers to come over and pick it up himself.

If one of his colleagues disagrees with him about how to apportion the towns and cities in a new sales region, he doesn't ask his colleague to submit a memorandum to him in which he makes a case for his point of view and then type up one of his own to submit in tandem to the vice-president for sales. What he does do is go to his colleague's office, close the door behind him, and ask his secretary not to put through incoming calls. And he doesn't leave until both of them have come to agreement. Another thing he doesn't do is to hash out such a problem over a three-hour lunch.

If he is given an assignment he doesn't quite understand, he tells his colleagues that he needs some help, and doesn't start changing things until he thinks he is competent to do so. What he especially doesn't do is hire some high-priced think tank to formulate a solution for him, which, even if it were right-minded, he would be too ignorant to appreciate.

In reward for his energetic and successful service, our Mr. Youthful has worked his way up to a vice-presidency. He is now middle-aged, rich, respected, and, unfortunately, the beneficiary of corporate luxury.

Now when two young managers from different divisions of his company come to him, both wanting to produce the new transistor equipment in their own division, he discovers that he can't see them because he has a board of directors meeting in the morning and in the afternoon he is speaking before the American Management Association on "The Dangers of Corporate Luxury." He asks the men to submit memoranda to him.

Being dutiful, both men do. It takes each of them about four hours to compose their presentation. Since one of the managers is an excellent writer and the other a lousy writer, the merits of the case are likely to become muddled.

Our vice-president receives the memos, but since he can now afford the most expensive advice, he brings in the management-expert team of Fixit, Chargeit, and Run. It takes the management experts two weeks to start working on the problem, and they ask the two competing division managers for a memorandum detailing what they want. Besides wasting another four hours of the managers' time, they have exacerbated their nerve endings and given them a sense of frustration and impotence. The management experts report back to the vice-president and he makes his decision, via a really nifty IBM personal portable dictaphone, while he is flying to London to meet the directors of the European subsidiary. He is unavailable for the reasonable rebuttal the defeated supplicant has ready. He is unaware that the whole affair has caused bad blood between two of his best managers, and he has put decision-making power in the hands of outsiders when it might effectively have been wielded from the inside.

Our important vice-president, however, feels proud of his ability to handle the problems of his subordinates while he is so busy. In the old days, he would have pushed both division managers into the empty board room, asked for their reasons verbally and made his decision right there, letting his intimate knowledge of the characters of both men have its full influence on him. And because it would have been highly likely that in the past month he would have been walking around the two competing divisions, he would already have been aware of the problem, and he would have been weighing subconsciously the exigencies of the decision with which he is now faced. His snap decision, would, in fact, be a considered one. Face-to-face contact would have defused any feelings of paranoia, and, lo and behold, our important executive would have discovered that he now had a whole day on his hands to solve other problems.

Townsend quotes Rabindranath Tagore: "All reality in life is relationship." That's what corporate luxury destroys.

The deleterious effects on the operations of a company ridden with corporate luxury are obvious, and any person experienced in business can provide scenarios alternative to the one Townsend has described. There is a moral consequence of such behavior, however, which is not obvious, but which I think is more insidious. Corporate luxury and the atrophy of relationships for which it is responsible make executives either unaware of or uncaring about the human consequences of their business decisions. I remember my shock when James Roche, the chief executive of General Motors, was quoted as having said as the sky was lit up by the flames from the riotous Detroit ghetto, "I never thought it could happen here." Incredible, isn't it? All you have to do is open your eyes and walk down a few streets in the Detroit urban ghetto or hear Detroit executives talk embarrassedly about their central city to realize that what was amazing about the Detroit riots was that they didn't happen sooner and that more damage wasn't done. The fact is, however, that corporate luxury often shields executives from having to see the unpleasant consequences of either the products they produce or the economic system which creates markets and profits for the producers of them. Michael Harrington, whose overall views leave me cold, speaks poignantly about the poor in his book *The Invisible Majority*. They are invisible to people who ride through the country on superhighways and in air-conditioned cars, people who think that Los Angeles and New York are summed up by the Beverly Hilton and the Carlyle. And to such people, what does the breakdown of urban transportation mean if more and more cars can be sold? After all, there is no traffic problem if you come to work at 10:30 and leave the driving to the chauffeur. Things never get too rushed or oppressive in Palm Beach either.

To any corporate client who I feel has the courage to enquire into what parts of his company are being shackled in efficiency and blinded to humanity by corporate luxury I will gladly devote my best efforts, and lend whatever help I can to his attempts at reform.

I have spoken about my fear that if corporations do not reform themselves, this country may undo the ties that bind:

the consent of the governed. I know of no more eloquent and powerful statement of the magnitude of the problems facing us than that enunciated by Barry Commoner in his book *The Closing Circle:*

> What is real in our lives is the apparently hopeless inertia of the economic and political system; its fantastic agility in sliding away from the basic issues which logic reveals; the selfish maneuvering of those in power, and their willingness to use, often unwittingly, and sometimes cynically, even environmental deterioration as a step toward more political power; the frustration of the individual citizen confronted by this power and evasion; the confusion that we all feel in seeking a way out of the environmental morass.
>
> Human beings have broken out of the circle of life, driven not by biological need, but by the social organization which they have devised to "conquer" nature: means of gaining wealth that are governed by requirements conflicting with those which govern nature. The end result is the environmental crisis, a crisis of survival. Once more to survive we must close the circle. We must learn how to restore to nature the wealth that we borrow from it.

Another hindrance to moral awakening in corporate life is what Paul Jacobson[2] calls "scientism" or "the appropriation of more-or-less scientific methodology to the study and manipulation of all events and, more importantly, the adopting of this methodology as the keystone of a pervasive world view, which leads to an inability to view any phenomena, including human and social, in other than empirical terms." Jacobson reminds us of the profound and widespread distrust

[2] Paul H. Jacobson, "No Room for Moral Values?" *The Wall Street Journal,* November 30, 1971.

of moral thought, especially among educated people who make up the establishment. Terms such as "subjective" or "biased" become pejorative. Respect is given only to assertions "firmly embedded in a matrix of 'facts' preferably rendered in a statistical format." Decisions on vital matters are deferred until the facts are in—facts "that may be hidden away in the drawers of some Byzantine Bureaucracy or are simply intellectually inaccessible to the trained mind."[3]

The establishment type who is most likely to act according to the directives of "scientism" Jacobson describes this way: "He has sacrificed his individuality to organization and institutionalization and has made a complete life style out of the forms of behavior condoned by a bureaucratized meritocracy; he is dedicated to the techniques of rational administration of life and is oriented toward reductionist 'problem solving' in all affairs; above all he is thoroughly 'pragmatic' and 'activist' and views with suspicion speculative thought not grounded in 'facts' and that does not lead to a 'program' for action."[4]

One of the buzz-words making the rounds in civic groups a couple of years ago was "action-research." One does not conduct research to gain answers. He must do research on which fund-raising action can be based.

The techniques of impersonal technology wielded by establishment types trained to act only on appropriate evidence often get applied to complex human situations, which are not at all susceptible to yielding the kind of quantifiable data on which a "scientific" decision can be made. Incidentally, this is one of the reasons for much of the conceptual poverty prevalent in today's behavioral "sciences." If a graduate student cannot subject his thesis question (hypothesis) to quantifiable testing and proof, he is usually told he cannot

---

[3] Jacobson, *Ibid.*
[4] *Ibid.*

make his hypothesis the subject of a thesis or dissertation because it does not conform to a "scientific" discipline. One only researches what he can quantify. Consequently, behavioral sciences, which purport in large measure to study the human condition, often end up answering questions nobody is asking.

Robert Kennedy thought that the big mistake Nikita Khrushchev had made in his calculation to arm Cuba with atomic missiles was that he could not *sense* that Americans would not tolerate an Eastern power's intervention in an area of influence Americans *consider* their own. That Americans do feel this way is not irrational; it is simply made up of a variety of influences so numerous and subtle that statistical analysis will not yield relevant conclusions. Robert McNamara's infamous game plan for Vietnam left out of the equation only the VC's dedication and the human consequences in psychological (as well as physical) damage that a purely military victory would require. City planners, typically dominated by the physical theories of architects and civil engineers rather than by those of professionals who make human interaction their focus, wonder why the shiny new high-rise developments that replace worn-out slums are subject to vandalism. They are cleaner, they are safer, they are cheaper—unfortunately, they don't make the people who live in them feel as if they have a home.

Because moral pronouncements or insights cannot be dressed up in the impressive trappings of "scientific" quantifications, those who seek to enthuse industry with the vigor of their insights often find their words falling on deaf ears. By default, the domain of moral pronouncement has been handed over to the "scientism" establishment. Jacobson cites a telling example:

> . . . We can listen to one expert expound on the propriety of wage-price controls, marshalling logical argument

and historical incident to their defense; on the other hand, another spokesman will argue, with seemingly equal logic and reference to facts, that such measures are doomed to failure.

However, once we identify the underlying *moral* assumptions, the mystery quickly falls away. In the former case, the *value* of social and economic security and harmony obviates almost any new coercive controls of the state; in the other case, the *value* of freedom from state coercion is so paramount that some social risk, insecurity and discord is a justifiable price to pay for it. In this light the facts, and the logical arguments by which they are processed, begin to take on the appearance of being largely a foil for advancing essentially moral assertions.[5]

Denys Munby, a reader in transportation economics at Nuffield College, Oxford, has written an article in *Commonweal* called "Morals and Measurements: Christian Ethics and Cost Benefit Analysis."[6] When my eye first took in the title, I was certain that I was about to read a spirited spoof of the pretensions of the moral "bookkeeper." But that's not what Munby had in mind at all.

He approaches the problem of the construction of a third airport for London. How much is the destruction of a site of beauty worth? He plays the role of cost-benefit analyst absolutely straight. He tries to assign value to beauty; to the loss to future generations; to the effect on the psyche; he tries to come up with an interest rate which will bridge the gap between what the cost of loss will be to this generation as opposed to future ones. The result is so complex, so bewildering; so apparently hopeless, that while we may regret

[5] Jacobson, *Ibid*.

[6] December 19, 1971, pp. 271–275.

that a well-meaning Christian statistician cannot assign book value to a moral issue, we rejoice that the reason he can't is the same reason we can't. Moral value doesn't yield to statistics.

At this point, in what I sense is bordering on polemic, I would love to be able to set forth a clear path for corporate action. I cannot. The battle to humanize our corporate methods will yield to no monolithic solutions. It would, of course, be sheer folly and the most uninformed idealism to expect or even want an end to *literal* corporate bureaucracy. After all, the literal meaning of bureaucracy is to organize men and tasks to meet objectives, and there certainly can be no substitute for that in any kind of human enterprise, be it corporate, civic, or communal. It is unfortunate that what often passes for bureaucracy in people's minds is precisely those dehumanizing factors of which I have been talking, so ubiquitous in corporate life, but having nothing to do with productive processes. It is mainly these sins of which the corporation should purge itself.

The corporation must be enjoined on many fronts and in the face of specific issues. One of the prime molders of the American economy is Wall Street and the men who manage the billions of dollars of investment capital entrusted to their care. The traditional purpose of a money manager in investing in the stock of a company is maximization of profit for his shareholders. This profit motive is the foundation of his fiduciary relationship to the investor. It has been an assumption of fund managers that it is not their job to seek corporate control in order to force changes of policy in any company. This is the spirit of the regulations defined in the SEC's rulings on the scope of mutual-fund operations.

The working relationship between corporate leadership and Wall Street has always been so intimate that no thinking member of either community would consistently think himself independent enough to ignore the activities of the other.

That interdependence, though, has historically been expressed in a dialogue almost exclusively limited to technical and financial data. There is a new breed of money manager growing up on Wall Street who will seriously modify that relationship. And he will do so by expressing his opinion loud and clear when he believes that a corporation is ignoring the crises of the times and persisting in patterns of behavior which threaten the welfare of the community.

This new breed recognizes that problems like air pollution will have to be met one way or another, and that only aggressive and imaginative efforts by the automotive and energy companies themselves will keep Government from imposing controls on their products. When management is doing little or nothing to protect its industry position, companies become unlikely investment targets. Traditionally attractive investments will cease to be attractive unless corporate management sees where the changing times will destroy old sources of income and where they will create the conditions for the discovery and exploitation of new ones.

Until recently, when its companies began to diversify actively, the tobacco industry had come under widespread and justified attack. To the new breed of money manager the tobacco industry couldn't be an attractive investment if it continued to make the cigarette business its only source of income. The plateau of tobacco securities several years ago bears witness to this truth. What many tobacco men began to recognize was that the time for diversification was upon them; spending millions to advertise an extra 15 mm. of the same health hazard no longer made sense. In the long run advertising money would be better spent on development and research, so that the corporation could find new ways to earn money and through diversification attract a new generation of bright young men eager to work for a management group which is keeping abreast of the times.

The investment community's feeling only a year or so ago was that the sole responsibility corporations have is to fatten the bottom line. The public outcry for public-spirited investments is changing that picture. As *Business Week* reports in its December 4, 1971, issue, "Now it seems that mutual fund investors prefer to have their money go into companies that care about ecology, minority hiring, and consumers. "Wellington Management Co. just got back 1,800 responses to a survey of investors who have $3.5 billion in Wellington's six funds. The survey showed that 82% believe the funds should emphasize investment in 'progressive and socially responsible companies,' and 89% believe that 'irresponsible corporations may end up paying a high price to correct past faults in such areas as pollution and product quality.' Curiously, shareholders over age 55 are more concerned about social issues than young investors, who prefer performance." (I guess that shows that the older ones may have made their pile and can now get onto more value-oriented concerns.) Wellington Management now "intends to send the survey results to all companies in its fund's portfolios. In case companies don't get the hint, the survey also shows that 97% of fund investors expect funds to apply pressure on social issues by voting proxies instead of deferring to management."

The Dreyfus Corporation has in SEC registry at this writing the Third Century Fund which will invest *only* in companies with progressive ecological and social records. As one prominent adviser to the fund summed it up, "The Third Century Fund was created so that we would invest only in the good guys."

I have a strong feeling that working for needed change in this country might not only result in long-term profit for the corporation but will make working a lot more fun than it has been for a long, long time.

Pressure for meaningful reform of corporation involvement

in social issues comes more forcefully from Government than from any other source. The complaints of the corporate world about Government's naiveté or heavy-handedness, or lack of sympathy and understanding, have in them a major share of truth. The sensible response to Government criticism, however, should not be a spiteful defensiveness toward what is wrong in the criticism or in the manner the remedies are administered, but a creative, industry-generated program for internal reform coupled with an industry-generated plan to cooperate with Government. If Government is too clumsy to administer reform, let industry show how it is better able to clean its own house. If Government is ignorant of the issues involved in corporate reform, let industry educate Government so that government is no longer ignorant. If there now exists a traditional enmity between the Government bureaucrat and the corporate executive, let them meet one another so that they may learn what one another are about.

One of the most encouraging steps in the direction of cementing a working relation between Washington and businessmen has been described in the October 16, 1971, issue of *Business Week*.[7]

Executive Interchange is "a federal experiment that taps promising executives from government and business for one-to-two-year assignments in the opposite sector." It is an "effort to build better understanding by bureaucrats and businessmen of each other's managerial problems . . .

"A group of 31 companies, including American Airlines, Atlantic Richfield, AT&T, Mobil Oil, Motorola, Bendix, Owens-Illinois, and Consolidated Edison are participating. The companies nominate promising executives for an interchange slot, and, in turn, agree to make jobs available for incoming government officials."

[7] P. 68.

The exchange managers have worked on such important projects as AT&T science research, a program on social responsibility for Norton Simon, Inc., and programs for the Environmental Protection Agency. The program executives are universally enthusiastic about the plan, but sound this warning note: "Keep in touch with your company. Some of the early participants did not, and after a year found that the corporate seas did not part on their return. We came into this program thinking our parent corporations were going to follow our progress for a year. Corporations just aren't that paternal. You've got to sell them on your skills when you come back."

Despite the problems of the program, Commission Director Joseph T. McCullen, Jr., sought to double participation in 1972 and get some of the "super-grade" Government executives involved.

As director, McCullen was on leave from Spencer Stuart & Associates. At the age of thirty-six he was acknowledged as one of the brightest young headhunters in America. His decision to become the recruiter for Executive Interchange is a virtue I hope my fellow headhunters will find it more worthy to emulate than to bask in.

No matter what variables are built into the business problems which confront a headhunter in the course of his career, the one invariable is people. Without a supply of the best minds and the most vigorous spirits, corporate life in America will stultify, unable to meet the challenges of change, becoming ever more separated from the citizenry who have traditionally identified more closely with business than with any other American institution. As in France, Italy, and Japan, the industrial elite will become a caste, rigidifying into an exclusive club unable and unwilling to put national interests alongside corporate ones. Young people must aspire to the corporate community or the corporate community will not be worth aspiring to. Despite turmoil and discontent, this may be the ripest moment in our history to yoke the concerns of the young to the operations of the corporation.

Never before in our history have students more forcefully demonstrated their willingness to participate in the decision-making processes of America's most important institutions, and never have they so forcefully demonstrated their refusal to be denied an effective role in these schemes.

At its most extreme, this student unrest has acted as judge and jury, convicting the instititions against which it acts of irremediable faults, and has therefore set itself in hostile, militant, and alien opposition to any cooperative plans for reform. This is the logic of the revolutionary, who will abrogate the most fundamental of American evolutionary guarantees—the guarantee of due process—to achieve his own vision of social justice. Before this vision, all the accumulated virtues of constitutional democracy are irrelevant: American democracy, American capitalism are malign, and in their place a new order must be ruthlessly established.

To the extent that this political credo is a plan for political action, it must be stopped with whatever legal and moral sanctions our Governmental and cultural heritage provide us, for these revolutionaries accuse society of a fascistic disregard for justice of which they themselves are the most gross practitioners.

To the extent, however, that this revolutionary militancy is a desperate measure, designed to point out our severe injustice, to shatter destructive complacency, and to mobilize America's energies for creative change, no American can afford to be deaf to its implications.

Obviously the world in which academia was a shaded grove has passed. F. Scott Fitzgerald's Princeton is a historical cameo; Oxford is more likely to produce a Harold Wilson than a Benjamin Jowett; and Jack Kennedys rather than Woodrow Wilsons seem likely to contend for the highest political offices of our nation.

Yet the academy has not perished with the age of genteel and leisured humanism. It flourishes and everywhere increases its power and influence. Presidents of major industrial complexes hold Ph.D.'s, Cabinet posts are filled with scholars; and except for small business, swelling ranks of technocrats have crowded the bold, self-educated entrepreneur from the deepest channels of the economic mainstream. In order to manage the complex organism that our nation has become, great intelligence and training are required. As our Governmental and industrial organizations grow more complex, the demand for skill grows correspondingly. And naturally this demand is filled largely through recruitment from the collegiate ranks. The power of business enterprise is so great that the relations between Government and business have never been more sensitive, and it is just because of capitalism's gigantic involvement with all that molds the American way of life that we must constantly check to see that what is essential to it is not pushed into the background by what is merely a means to our spiritual, moral, and political ends.

If there is collegiate dissatisfaction with the aims of our industrial state, which causes reluctance or outright refusal to cooperate in the major projects of our country, the problem becomes—obviously enough—more than collegiate; it becomes national.

When John Kenneth Galbraith was describing the components of the new industrial state, he pointed out that the control of productivity has passed into the hands of the decision-making organisms of five or six hundred giant corporations. The five hundred largest of these account for over two-thirds of all manufacturing assets, and three hundred and eighty-four of them account for 85 percent of the expenditures made for industrial research and development.

The technological requirements of such vast organizations

are equally vast, requiring specialized knowledge from experts in dozens of technical fields. There must be market strategists and industrial planners who predict consumer demand, and who must foresee, during the years of a product's development, variations in labor costs and plant locations, Government policy, the price of raw materials, etc. Finally, there is the need for an organization which will coordinate all this information.

The organism of which these complex structures are a part Galbraith terms the "technostructure." And it is the needs of this technostructure which have placed an unprecedented demand and premium on the knowledge of our academies. Yet at the precise moment in our history when that demand has reached its peak, resistance to it has peaked on our campuses.

Certainly one of the most relevant facts about this generation of young Americans is that they are for the most part protected from the economic preoccupations of nutrition, shelter, and leisure which often haunted their mothers and fathers.

The pride which older generations took in establishing their economic security is justified, and in no place but America was a reward for their honest labor offered. What a great luxury it is, therefore, to see the sons of these fathers proclaiming that economic emancipation is not their preoccupation, and, that, in fact, to make it a central consideration in their lives is to misunderstand their vision of American democracy. This is quite a gift America has made, in spite of the sadness it has caused between the generations.

But Americans on all wave lengths of the political spectrum must recognize this: that America is a political idea, not an economic one; that we are a constitutional democracy above and beyond all else; and a capitalistic economy importantly, but not essentially.

Students have come to believe that the industrial-governmental hegemony has confused the demands of economic well-being with democratic well-being, and in the process is diverting so much of its energies to the pursuit of affluence and national pride that it neglects the social and moral imperatives which would require every American to ration his demands on America's superabundance.

What is relevant in student protest, therefore, is not its disdain for wealth, but the way it is being spent; is not its disdain for political power, but its alienation from the centers of intellect and compassion; and, finally, it is not a rejection of American politics, but of the extraneous wheeling and dealing which pervert its quick and just function.

In fact, American capitalism has been and continues to be the most effective producer of wealth in a free society; yet its value to America must never be judged in terms of its economic bounty alone. For when that bounty becomes inimical to the aims of democratic government and the assumptions about the dignity of its citizens on which it is based, it is Mammon's feast.

It is ironic that so much resentment is borne by the producers of this nation's material wealth; for, throughout the world, there is a deepening sense that individuals, communities, and nations have much more ability to get things done than they used to have. This ability to move where we want to go—or ought to go—is called power, and this power is largely the product of our technological advances.

For many of the older generations, demands for Black Power are more cogent than the cry for power which their well-fed, well-educated sons and daughters are raising; for this cry is not for material benefits as much as it is for political and ultimately moral ones.

While lawless militancy is the most dramatic and most odious example of student discontent, it is not the most significant nor the most widespread. The wills of this present generation have not been shaped, as were the fathers', as much for acquisition as for public service, and their inclination is to shy away from traditional sources of prestige and power, which they see as enemies hostile to that ambition.

The scions of some of America's great industrial fortunes are the most dramatic testimony to this change of ambition. Carnegies, Rockefellers, Kennedys, Harrimans, and Roosevelts no longer find the industrial aggrandizement of their fortunes sufficient justification for citizenship. And in households all across the country the poignant tale of the family business, built with nothing but the family's toil, and now left without an heir, is enacted every day.

This generation's discontent is not only an indication that there is something wrong with American society; it is clear evidence that our young citizens are unwilling to live off the abundance of a land in which they see ingrained injustice and moral complacency.

I have been stressing the alienation of the collegian from the industrial enterprise, and trying to show how and why it has happened, because industry has become so influential that alienation from it is in fact alienation from the mainstream of our society.

No matter how often we are told that poverty and racial injustice in this country are the concerns of the first national priority, the message doesn't seem to take hold. Have we evolved so far from our original democratic belief in equal opportunity that our political self-righteousness is no more based on moral verities than the political cant of any powerful nation seeking to justify its acquisitiveness? This is what our young are wondering about. The speculation is not idle.

Toward the end of his life, Edmund Burke, who had eloquently and consistently denounced the French Revolution, looked back at his opposition to it, and in a memorandum containing some of the last pages he ever wrote said:

If a great change is to be made in human affairs, the minds of men will be fitted to it; the general opinions and feelings will draw that way. Every fear, every hope will forward it; and then they who persist in opposing this mighty current in human affairs, will appear rather to resist the decrees of Providence itself, than the mere designs of men. They will not be resolute and firm, but perverse and obstinate.

I believe that the discontent of our young heralds such a current as Burke describes, and it will not do to dismiss it by concentrating on what is frivolous, stupid, or misdirected in it. Because carried along with all that can be dismissed without harmful consequence is a political and moral message for our nation, which, if we fail to heed and act upon it, will make us witnesses to the failure of the traditions we have most dearly cherished.

ABOUT THE AUTHOR

ALLAN J. COX is a consultant on problems of business management and President of the Chicago executive search firm Management Organization, Inc. A graduate of Northern Illinois University with a B.A. in Social Science and a Master's degree in Sociology, Mr. Cox was an Associate Consultant with Case and Company and Spencer Stuart & Associates, and Vice President of Westcott Associates before founding his own firm in 1969. *Confessions of a Corporate Headhunter* grew out of his experiences in recruiting key executives for America's top managerial positions. A portion of the book appeared earlier in *Playboy*. Mr. Cox is married, the father of a six-year-old daughter, and lives in Chicago.